THE NEW MERMAIDS

Eastward Ho!

Eastward Ho!

BEN JONSON
GEORGE CHAPMAN
JOHN MARSTON

Edited by C. G. PETTER

ERNEST BENN LIMITED
LONDON

First published in this form 1973
by Ernest Benn Limited
Sovereign Way · Tonbridge · Kent
© *Ernest Benn Limited 1973*
Distributed in Canada by
The General Publishing Company Limited · Toronto
Printed in Great Britain
ISBN 0 510-33310-9
Paperback 0 510-33311-7

TO
RANDOLPH STOW

CONTENTS

Acknowledgements   ix

List of Abbreviations   xi

Introduction   xiii

    Authorship   xiii

    Date and Sources   xxiii

    The Play   xxvii

    Stage History   xxxvii

    Note on The Text   xxxix

    Further Reading   xlvii

EASTWARD HO!   1

    Dramatis Personae   3

    Prologue   5

    Text   7

    Epilogue   118

Appendix 1   A Map of London   120

Appendix 2   An anonymous ballad relating to forty-pound knights   123

Appendix 3   Imprisonment—The Letters Written by Chapman and Jonson from Prison   125

Appendix 4   First Quarto Press Corrections   133

ACKNOWLEDGEMENTS

NO MODERN EDITOR of *Eastward Ho!* could fail to pay tribute to the Oxford editors, C. H. Herford, P. and E. Simpson, for the exemplary scholarship of their textual and critical commentaries on the play (*Ben Jonson*, II, IV, and IX). A second, and no less important, textual reference was the C. F. Brooke and N. Paradise edition in *English Drama 1580–1642* (Boston, 1933), pp. 397–435. Other sources of critical insight are included in *Further Reading* (see below, p. xlvii).

I would like to thank Professor Andrew Gurr for his guidance and encouragement throughout my initial research. At later stages, David Paul, Timothy Vernon, David O'Neill, John Ross, Professor Arthur Brown, and my mentor, Mr John Horden, all contributed valuable suggestions. Responsibility for any omission is, needless to say, entirely mine.

I should like to thank Diana Herbert for her tireless attention to my typescripts, and finally to The Canada Council I owe a special debt of thanks for their generous research fellowship.

London   C. G. P.

June 1972

LIST OF ABBREVIATIONS

ed.	this editor.
Ed.	an earlier editor.
H. & S.	C. H. Herford, P. & E. Simpson, eds., *Ben Jonson.* 11 vols., Oxford, 1925–52.
MLN	*Modern Language Notes.*
MP	*Modern Philology.*
N&Q	*Notes and Queries.*
N.E.D.	*New English Dictionary.*
O.E.D.	*Oxford English Dictionary.*
PQ	*Philological Quarterly.*
Q	copy text.
Qq	all copies of first quarto.
Q2	second quarto, BM 644 d53.
Q3	third quarto.
SB	*Studies in Bibliography.*
s.d.	stage direction.
s.p.	speech prefix.
SP	*Studies in Philology.*
Tilley	M. P. Tilley, ed., *A Dictionary of Proverbs in England in the Sixteenth and Seventeenth Centuries*, Ann Arbor, 1950.

INTRODUCTION

AUTHORSHIP

EARLY ATTEMPTS to identify the precise contributions of the three collaborators of *Eastward Ho!* were made on the basis of intuition, tempered by a knowledge of the plays solely the work of Marston, Chapman, and Jonson individually. Early conjectures such as J[ames] C[rossley]'s in *Blackwood's Edinburgh Magazine* (September 1821) and F. G. Fleay's (*Biographical Chronicle of the English Drama*, 1891) speculate boldly on the division of authorship without a shred of supporting evidence. Twentieth-century studies of the problem have been less arbitrary and more willing to concede the difficulty of solving the riddle by comparative analysis of verbal parallels between the unaided plays and *Eastward Ho!* A. H. Bullen and F. E. Schelling considered the question insoluble and suggested that studies of verbal similarities were a waste of ingenuity. Percy Simpson, one of the editors of the Oxford *Ben Jonson*, hit on the crux of the problem when he wrote: 'from the beginning of the seventeenth century there was a tendency for individual dramatic styles in prose dialogue to converge on one more or less established type . . .', so that the desire to press home verbal parallels may lead the critic far from the actuality of authorship.[1] The studies accompanying the editions of Professor Cunliffe in C. M. Gayley's *Representative English Comedies* (1913) and of Dr Julia H. Harris in the Yale Studies in English (series no. 73; 1926) demonstrate the weaknesses of an argument based entirely on syntax. Both came to the conclusion that Jonson had no direct part in the writing, a theory which later studies, including my own, thoroughly refute. Criteria such as 'sentence structure' and 'alliteration' are unfortunately too arbitrary to apply in judging prose which selfconsciously parodies literary styles of the day.

The most definitive studies of the authorship problem to date are to be found in Professor Parrott's edition of *The Plays and Poems of George Chapman: The Comedies* (1913) and in Simpson's textual introduction in *Ben Jonson* (H. & S., IX; 1950). Both Parrott and Simpson base their divisions on parallel passages, consistency of

---

[1] H. & S., IX, 637.

characterization, and an intuitive detection of that 'perhaps indefinable but unmistakable tone and flavour peculiar to an author'.[2] They are both accomplished scholars and well qualified by their years of editing to make such assessments. Inductive argument, nevertheless, is always open to question, particularly when conclusions from two such studies are contradictory in some respects. The chief difference between the two analyses arises from Professor Parrott's contention that 'no one familiar with the conditions under which the Elizabethan drama was produced can believe that three playwrights of that day worked together on a scene, mutually contributing, criticizing, and elaborating'.[3] Simpson appears to reject this theory by assigning several scenes to more than one author.

External evidence favours Simpson's decision to look for more than one hand in a scene. Jonson told Drummond that 'he was delated [informed on] by Sir James Murray to the King for writting something against the Scots in a play Eastward hoe, and voluntarly Imprissonned himself *with* Chapman and Marston, who had written it amongst *them*'.[4] The ambiguous 'it' has been interpreted variously as the particular passage containing the offensive satire or earlier acts and scenes put together in Jonson's absence. Chapman's plea to the king that 'the chief offences are but two clauses, and both of them not our own',[5] seems to pin the responsibility for the gibe (III, iii, 38–45) on Marston although critics have almost universally assigned the rest of the scene to Chapman himself.

Recent research has uncovered an interesting statement about the methods of seventeenth-century collaboration which qualifies Parrott's theory of independent contribution by showing that some scenes had a composite origin. Professor C. J. Sisson found Dekker's 1624 testimony concerning material he contributed to a play involving Rowley, Ford, and Webster. Dekker said that he wrote 'two sheetes of paper conteyning the first Act, and a speech in the last Scene of the last Act'. Sisson's conclusion is

that the play was jobbed out to the four authors in detached acts, with one important passage at least reserved for special treatment . . . Doubtless the need for rapid production dictated this multiplicity

[2] T. M. Parrott, ed., *The Plays and Poems of George Chapman: The Comedies* (London, 1913), 843.
[3] ibid. (See *Authorship Table* (below, p. xxi) for a summary of Parrott's and Simpson's Divisions of Authorship.)
[4] 'Conversations with Drummond', H. & S., I, 140.
[5] See Appendix 3, Letter I. (But the printer appears to have cut three 'clauses' and cancelled a further one, so it is impossible to know which 'two clauses' actually caused the offence.)

of authorship, and precluded anything in the shape of close continuous collaboration between all four.[6]

Although only three authors were involved in *Eastward Ho!*, there can be little doubt that it was produced in a similar way and for the same reason.

With external evidence of authorship so negligible, a division of authorship must depend on internal evidence. Professor Cyrus Hoy, in a series of seven articles in *Studies in Bibliography* (1956–62), has illustrated the effectiveness of counting abbreviations as a means of detecting authorship. By tabulating the linguistic preferences of authors who worked on the Beaumont and Fletcher canon, he was able, with some measure of accuracy, to divide the plays between their collaborators. In the course of this study Professor Hoy touched on the linguistic habits of Chapman and Jonson in *Rollo of Normandy*. Hoy's study of *Rollo* revealed that Jonson's habits of abbreviation differed so remarkably from Chapman's as to make evidence of authorship both tangible and accessible. For 'them' Jonson regularly writes ''hem', while Chapman prefers the forms ''em', ''am', or ''um'; Jonson uses 'i'the' and 'o'the' for 'of the' while Chapman sets 'i'th'', 'o'th'', and occasionally 'a'th''. Jonson infrequently employs the form 'yo'' for 'you' while Chapman substitutes 'y''; Chapman sometimes uses 'an't' for 'on it' or 'of it'.

The scope of Professor Hoy's study was not great enough to allow an appraisal of *Eastward Ho!*, and though he makes a few suggestions for assignment,[7] he does so without defining Marston's habitual abbreviations and therefore without sufficient accuracy. Both to substantiate Hoy's findings and to define Marston's preferences, I have devised a table including most of the unaided comedies written by the three authors between 1599 and 1610, three of which were published by George Eld, the printer of *Eastward Ho!* (see below, Table 1, p. xx). It would be as well to say here that the likelihood of this test defining compositorial habits rather than authorial ones is lessened both by the compositor analysis (see below, *Note on the Text*, p. xli) and by a selection of plays from a number of different printing shops. The consistency with which abbreviations appear within different early quartos of the same playwright must provide undeniable proof of authorship.

Marston's linguistic peculiarities are less easy to describe than Jonson's or Chapman's. They are remarkable chiefly for their

---

[6] C. J. Sisson, *Lost Plays of Shakespeare's Age* (Cambridge, 1936), p. 112.
[7] C. Hoy, 'The Shares of Fletcher and His Collaborators in the Beaumont and Fletcher Canon, VI', *SB*, XIV (1961), 61–3.

scarcity. Nonetheless he uses two forms not used by the others: 'ha' without an apostrophe and 'a the' (found six times in *The Dutch Courtesan*); 'a your', 'a my', 'tho', and numerals appear more frequently in Marston's plays. Other mutually exclusive criteria not set forth by Professor Hoy are Chapman's use of 'ahlas', and the absence of the 'de' ending for 'ed' (frequently substituted by Marston and Chapman) in Jonson.

In view of linguistic preference it is possible to corroborate the earlier studies based on style, of which Simpson's is recognized as definitive. The test confirms that the First Act is Marston's: 'ha' appears seven times without an apostrophe, 'tho' is found four times, and 'a the' occurs on sig. B1^r. The lengthy stage directions and rhymed tags are further evidence of Marston's hand.[8] Lengthy stage directions of II, i indicate that Marston began the Second Act as well. Professor Hoy believes that the 'an'him' abbreviation on sig. B2^v indicates Chapman, but as the exact phrase is 'off an'him' (avoiding the awkwardness of 'off of him') such an ascription is dubious. The abbreviations 'a their', 'a'your', 'a,my' (twice), and the extended form 'you are' (twice) point to Marston as sole author of this scene.

The awkwardness of Security's speech opening II, ii marks, as Herford notes, a sudden transition to a more elevated and dignified style.[9] It is an obvious hinge to the earlier scenes and creaks noticeably. The stage direction which starts the scene, '*Security solus*', is exactly that of *All Fools* ('*Rinaldo solus*', sig. H3^r) and the abbreviations which follow are certainly Chapman's. 'Ahlas', 'an't' (meaning 'of it'), and 'a'th' occur, and 'de' is found regularly instead of 'ed'.[10] Similarly II, iii can be assigned to Chapman on the basis of 'y'ad' and 'ha''; and because, as G. Cross notes, 'foisting' (55) is a common Chapman word.[11] The passage after Security's entrance with Sindefy

---

[8] The work of Gustav Cross confirms this assignment. See G. Cross, 'Some Notes on the Vocabulary of John Marston', *N&Q* (1954–63). Cross believes that Marston coined the following words: 'gallanted' I, i, 42 (1959, p. 102); 'bavin' I, i, 69 (1955, p. 20); 'ill-natured' I, i, 83 (1961, p. 125); 'flash' I, i, 87 (1957, p. 223); 'daringly' I, ii, 167, 'court-amble' I, ii, 61, 'court sport' I, ii, 84, 'court-cut' I, i, 82 (1960, p. 135); 'dunghill' I, i, 91 (1956, p. 471); 'canvas-backed' I, i, 110 (1960, p. 135).

[9] H. & S., II, 45.

[10] Dr J. I. Cope, '*Volpone* and the Authorship of *Eastward Hoe*', *MLN*, LXXII (1957), 253–6, attributes this scene to Jonson on parallels between Security's soliloquy and Mosca's speech, I, i, 33–9 (H. & S., V). It is possible that Jonson sketched the scene for Chapman, or that he revised it to remove an offence on C1^v–C2^r of Q.

[11] G. Cross, op. cit. (1959), 254.

(102) is possibly Marston's, both for the reasons given by Simpson; because 'you are' replaces Chapman's form 'y'are'; and because, as Cross notes, 'acceptation' (138) is a Marston word.[12]

It is difficult to assign the short scene III, i solely in the light of linguistic preference. Only one 'de' occurs and this occurs in the passage assigned to Jonson by the Oxford editors. (Parrott is probably right about the scene being entirely Chapman's.) Even more difficult is the problem raised by III, ii, which Simpson divides between the three authors: Marston 1–82, Jonson 83–196, and Chapman 197–336. The evidence of linguistic preferences here reveals that the scene is entirely Chapman's. The occurrence of 'in's', 'ith'', and 'Ahlas' (twice) marks 1–82 as Chapman's; in the middle section, 'te'ye', a 'de', and 'a'my' point to Chapman; and the last passage is his by virtue of the 'de' ending, 't'' in 't'advise', and the spelling 'Billingsgate' for Jonson's 'Belingsgate'. III, iii also I assign to Chapman, including the 'Scots' passage, which contains the distinctive Chapman form 'an't' for 'of it', and 'ahlas' twice. It would be impossible on the basis of linguistic preference to assign the five lines of III, iv, which Simpson gives to Marston.

Act IV, scene i again has little linguistic evidence to help us determine authorship. 1–112 is probably Marston's; 'Alas' occurs four times and the peculiar 'A, my' (used by Marston in II, i) recurs here as does 'a'that'. The verse passage 113–32, usually assigned to Chapman, has only one 'de' ending to distinguish it. The change from 'them' to ''hem' (used eight times) in 133–230, and the 'o'the' (used twice) mark this passage, which includes the gentlemen's humiliation of Petronel and the alchemical jargon, as Jonson's. Finally, 231–82, which has an 'Ahlas', and the final speech of Slitgut which resembles the encomium on the horn in *All Fools*, I assign to Chapman. The obvious inconsistencies of characterization in this scene confirm the above division.

IV, ii and V throughout bear irrefutable evidence of Jonson's authorship.[13] 'de', which occurred twenty times for 'ed' in earlier scenes, does not occur at all from IV, ii on. On the other hand 'o'the', 'i'the', and 'ha'' are found in unprecedented numbers; 'o'the' thirteen, 'i'the' fourteen, 'ha'' nine times. The distinctive Jonson spellings 'Belingsgate' and 'you 'are' also occur in Act V. Only in one speech, IV, ii, 215–39 (where Touchstone recapitulates Quicksilver's history of crime), does a trace of Marston's hand appear. Here numerals occur thrice, as well as 'a'my', suggesting that Marston contributed these lines to Jonson's scene in order to improve cohesion.

The authorship of the *Prologue* and the *Epilogue*, probably added at the time of the first performance, is difficult to determine. 'De' appears twice for 'ed' in the *Prologue*, perhaps indicating that it is not Jonson's, as Parrott and Simpson think. The assignment of the *Prologue* to Chapman on the basis of verbal parallels with the prologue of *Bussy D'Ambois* is not an attractive possibility,[14] since the latter belongs to the 1641 Q and has never seriously been ascribed to Chapman. Marston's close connection with the Queen's Revels makes the ascription to him the most plausible.

The system of capitalization, punctuation, and use of italic type varies throughout the *Eastward Ho!* Quarto and is difficult to identify with any of the three authors. The only evidence indicating that one hand may have been responsible for the manuscript is the ubiquitous ''hem' (Jonson's abbreviation for 'them'), which occurs thirty-three times throughout the play. Otherwise, discrepancies in spelling (other than compositorial) and the appearance of the peculiar spellings 'Ahlas' and 'Gould' (found rarely outside the Chapman canon) indicate that a large part of the printer's copy was in Chapman holograph. It is possible that Jonson revised the work of the other two collaborators, but I think it far more likely, knowing the high standards that Jonson set for his written work, that the printer's copy was a scribal copy of work submitted independently by all three authors.

The division of authorship by linguistic analysis confirms that Sisson's comments about the methods of collaboration can be applied to *Eastward Ho!* Each author wrote one large section and contributed a short piece or pieces to scenes devised by another author. Hence Marston wrote I and II, i independently, contributed short pieces to II, iii, IV, i, and V, iii, and added the *Prologue* and *Epilogue* when the play was first staged. Chapman wrote most of II, ii to III, iii and two short pieces for IV, i; he may have added Security's opening speech as an afterthought. Jonson's share was a small section of IV, i (133–230) and the whole of IV, ii and V, excepting the speeches added by Marston and Chapman for cohesion. (Jonson may have also supervised the revision of E3^v–E4^r—of the three authors he alone uses 'inough' and 'enough' with equal frequency, and it is he who so liberally uses proverbs in the last Act.) Altogether the method of collaboration would have allowed the three authors to write different sections of the play simultaneously. This must explain the

---

[14] See H. D. Sykes, 'The Prologue To Jonson, Chapman and Marston's *Eastward Hoe*', *N&Q*, XI (Jan. 1915), 5–6.

INTRODUCTION xix

apparent haste with which the text was assembled (see below, *Note on the Text*, p. xl) and the fluidity and speed with which the play moves.[15]

Although modern editors believe that *Eastward Ho!* was Marston's idea it is hard, as Parrott says, 'not to see Jonson's hand in the careful planning and admirable adjustment of the whole'.[16] This method of structuring the plot on opposites is most Jonsonian, Marston preferring the disguise plot.[17] Typical too is the creation of characters after alchemical or humour models (Touchstone's household) and on the basis of their economic position (Security's brood). The use of ingenious stage devices to exemplify the moral, as in the Cuckold's Haven scene, is a technique which established Jonson as the foremost masque writer of his day. Chapman and perhaps Marston had worked for Jonson before, and it is difficult to imagine the enterprise not taking shape under the direction of the most experienced and outspoken playwright of the three.

Eastward Ho! is acknowledged as one of the most successful collaborations written for the Jacobean stage—and rightly so. It combines the abilities of the three most talented coterie dramatists in a well wrought and brilliantly vivid city comedy free from the excesses and spleen of their earlier unaided works. Marston's deft sharp sketching and vigorous handling of dialogue put the play in

[15] R. M. Wren, *The Blackfriars Theatre and Its Repertory, 1600–1608*, Princeton University Microfilms, unpublished PhD. thesis, 1965, p. 230, demonstrates how this kind of division works with the character of Quicksilver:

'1. To Marston—he is a rebellious fool (I, II, i, IV, i)
2. To Chapman—he is an accomplished secondary to Sir Petronel's plot (something of the clever slave of Roman comedy) (II, III)
3. To Jonson—he is a leader and upholder of spirits in adversity (late IV, i, IV, ii, V)'.

[16] Parrott, op. cit., 843.
[17] *The Dutch Courtesan* (Marston) was dated by E. K. Chambers (*The Elizabethan Stage*, Oxford, 1923, III, 430) as 1603–04. The fact that it has a similar plot structure to *Eastward Ho!* has been the principal argument for Marston's plot direction. Anthony Caputi (*John Marston Satirist*, N.Y., 1961, pp. 217–40) rejects Chambers's date for *The Dutch Courtesan*, which he thinks was written at the same time as or after *Eastward Ho!* P. J. Finkelpearl (*John Marston of the Middle Temple*, Cambridge, Mass., 1969, p. 197n.) concurs with Caputi's date but rejects his conclusion, i.e. that Marston learned the double-plot structure from the collaboration. Finkelpearl suggests 'that *Eastward Hoe* is built on a structure of contrasts similar to that... already employed in *Jack Drum's Entertainment*. . . .' I would counter that the resemblance of plot and structure to Jonson's *Every Man in His Humour* (1598) is far more marked.

motion. In Chapman's scenes, which make up the subplot, the motivations are carefully balanced until the intriguers sway drunkenly in anticipation of the malice they have worked. Finally Jonson, whose careful plotting permeates and unites the play, allows the characters gradually to find their own balance, with a genial detachment which fosters parody and prepares the triumph of comedy over didacticism.

Table 1: Abbreviations in Plays by Marston, Chapman, and Jonson

	'em/am/um	'hem	i'th	i'the	a'th	o'th	o'the	ha	ha'	inough	enough	de	Ahlas	an/on, of	t'	yo'
MARSTON																
Jack Drum								5		2	3	40			1	
Dutch C.	1		1					22		4	7	26				
Fawne								36		3	8	43				
*W.Y.W.								18		5		1				
CHAPMAN																
M.D'Ol.	12		3		5						4	18	5	3	1	
Gent. Ush.	4		1			1			4	2	8	41	1		18	
May Day	45	2	7			7	1	1			8	2			5	10
W's Tears	1		4			9	1				6				7	6
*All Fools	10		1	1	3					1	10	15	9	1	18	
JONSON																
*Sej.		19	1	1		1	1	2	13	1					8	5
Epic.		103	1	35			32	31	5	3					4	5
Alchem.		47		34			42	80	2	6					4	5
Volp.		42	3	5	4	6	31	2	2						6	11

* indicates these plays printed by George Eld, the printer of *Eastward Ho!*

Titles

Marston: *Jack Drum's Entertainment* (1600), *The Dutch Courtesan* (1605), *The Fawne* (1604), *What You Will* (1601).

Chapman: *Monsieur D'Olive* (1604), *The Gentleman Usher* (1602?), *May Day* (1602?), *Widow's Tears* (c. 1605), *All Fools* (1604?).

Jonson: *Sejanus* (1603), *Epicœne* (1609), *The Alchemist* (1610), *Volpone* (1606).

Table 2: Division of Authorship

	Parrott		Simpson		Petter	
Design+Plotting		M + J		M		J
Prologue		J		J		M
I, i		M		M		M
I, ii		M		M		M
II, i		M	1–49	J		M
			50–81	M		
			82–133	J		
			134–63	M		
II, ii		M r J		C		C
II, iii		C + M	1–87	C	1–101	C
			88–160	M	102–60	M
III, i		C	1–36	J		C
			37–66	C		
III, ii	1–203	C + M	1–82	M		C
	204–336	C	83–196	J		
			197–336	C		
III, iii		C		C		C
III, iv		M		M		M
IV, i		C r J	1–112	M	1–112	M
			113–74	C	113–32	C
			175–267	J	133–230	J
			268–82	M	231–282	C
IV, ii		M r J		J	1–214	J
					215–39	M
					240–319	J
V, i		M r J		J		J
V, ii		J		J		J
V, iii		J		J		J
V, iv		J		J		J
V, v		J	1–191	J		J
			192–7	M		
Epilogue		J		M		M

r = revised by

DATE AND SOURCES

The Prologue of *Eastward Ho!* replies to *Westward Ho!* which critics agree was produced in the winter of 1604.[18] This is the inside limit for the writing of *Eastward Ho!* The Stationers' Register date of 4 September 1605 forms the outside limit for production. *Eastward Ho!* was probably first produced midway between these limits, during the king's Greenwich sojourn, mid-March to mid-June 1605. Both internal and external evidence points to it. First the topical reference of Quicksilver's motto gives the play its title. During the spring of 1605, when London was swamped with would-be gallants flocking to the Court of James I, the Thames waterman's cry of 'Eastward Ho!' must have become synonymous with pursuing favour at Court. Hence, the gullible Quicksilver has taken up the cry, and likewise the ambition: 'I'll to the Court, another manner of place for maintenance, I hope, than the silly City!' (II, ii, 54–5). This also lends weight to A. H. Bullen's conjecture that the anonymous gentleman who derides Sir Petronel on the Isle of Dogs 'mimicked James's Scotch accent' (IV, i, 163–8). This association would follow if he was in residence just opposite, at Greenwich Palace. Such scandalous scenes would also fit Samuel Calvert's complaint of 28 May 1605, that:

> The Plays do not forbear to present upon their Stage the whole Course of this present Time, not sparing either King, State, or Religion, in so great Absurdity, and with such Liberty, that any would be afraid to hear them.[19]

Apart from this letter, there is no documented evidence of the official reaction to the play, and whether it was the staging or the later publication which constituted the offence. The orthodox view is that publication was the offence for which cancellation witnesses the redress. But, as Dr W. W. Greg wrote, 'perhaps no certain conclusion is possible on the evidence before us'.[20] The evidence to which

---

[18] E. K. Chambers, op. cit., III, 254–6.

[19] Samuel Calvert to Sir Ralph Winwood, *Winwood's Memorials* (London, 1725), II, 54. Another of Calvert's letters, dated 6 April 1605, states: 'that there is now a compleat court at *Greenwich* for some Months'. The king was there at tilting on 24 March.

[20] W. W. Greg, ' "Eastward Ho" 1605', *Library*, IX (1928), 303–4.

he refers is the letters written by Jonson and Chapman from prison, included in Appendix 2 of this edition. Nevertheless, the internal evidence that certain offensive passages were expunged by the publisher prompted Dr J. Q. Adams to challenge the accepted theory in 1931.[21] Adams drew three important conclusions: (1) that the publisher revised the text in proof, and on his own authority; (2) that the publication was the authors' 'justification' for the offence; and (3) that the imprisonment was therefore a direct result of the play's production.

On the first point, the *Note on the Text* (below, p. xliii) conjectures that the text might well have been revised in proof. But from the other points these questions arise: if the printing was a 'justification' why did the authors not preface the play with a defence of their innocence (as was done for Jonson's *Volpone*, 1606, and Marston's *The Fawn*, 1606)? And secondly, would not a printer whom Adams describes as 'economical', even 'niggardly', have the foresight to edit the MSS. rather than go through the wasteful process of editing in the press and then cancelling?

My own bibliographic study suggests the possibility that the printers were startled; composition was interrupted to make the corrections before the formes went to press. In the scramble to correct Q one topical clause (III, iii, 38–45) and a number of minor quips completely escaped, and E3ʳ–E4ᵛ had to be cancelled after the first sales had begun. I am convinced that it could only have been the furore surrounding the authors' imprisonment that caused the printer so much trouble. Surely, had any of the authors been available, they could have readily supplied the publisher with the necessary stop-gaps.

But there still remains one unanswered question. Why did the king's anger descend on the playwrights in September rather than at the time of the original production? To this I believe R. E. Brettle has the answer.[22] He conjectures that an unlicensed production of *Eastward Ho!*, perhaps with satirical additions from the actors, was performed while the king was on his Oxford Progress (July–September 1605). A similar offence caused the dissolution of the Blackfriars company in 1608.[23] He also cites from Chapman's letter to the Lord Chamberlain (II, Appendix 3, pp. 126–7): 'our unhappy book was presented without your Lordship's allowance' . . . because 'our play

[21] J. Q. Adams, '*Eastward Hoe* and its Satire Against the Scots', *SP*, XXVIII (1931), 157–69.

[22] R. E. Brettle, '*Eastward Ho*, 1605; by Chapman, Jonson, and Marston; Bibliography and Circumstances of Production', *The Library*, IX (1928–29), 287–302.

[23] Chambers, op. cit., II, 53–4 and Brettle, op. cit., p. 299.

[was] so much importuned' . . . when 'your Person [was] so far removed
from our required attendance'. Both the Lord Chamberlain and the
official censor, Samuel Daniel, probably accompanied the king to
Oxford.

Brettle's view that it was an unlicensed performance, during the
summer, that had rumours wildly circulating when the king returned
to Whitehall in mid-September, conforms with both the external
and internal evidence. The play had been legally licensed and
printing had begun when the trouble broke. Marston, the most
intimately associated with the production, caught wind of it and
escaped. His fellow shareholder in the company, Edward Kirkham,
also thought it prudent to dissociate himself from the play, and did
so by changing allegiance to Paul's Boys before he was dragged into
the affair.[24]

The source of the main plot is still unknown, although previous
editors from Schelling on have pointed to similarities with the
prodigal son school plays: *Acolastus*, a Latin school-play in Henry
VIII's reign; *The Nice Wanton*, an interlude from the succeeding
reign; *Misogonus* (*c.* 1560–77) and Ingcland's *The Disobedient Child*
(*c.* 1560). These plays were used to demonstrate the rewards of economic prudence. The later public moralities, Gascoigne's *The Glass of
Government* (*c.* 1575) and *The London Prodigal* (*c.* 1604), attempted to
update the theme by placing the play in a contemporary milieu. This
anticipates *Eastward Ho!* though here the emphasis shifts from
didacticism to satiric burlesque, so that the theme is transformed
into a comedy of manners in which 'the old plays on Prodigals are
mocked with a straight face'.[25]

The subplot depends on the elements of Terentian comedy. The
intrigue derives from Masuccio's *Il Novellino* No. 40 (1475);[26] references to Virginia are drawn from More's *Utopia* and Hakluyt's
Voyages; and a passage in Act V comes from Rabelais's *Pantagruel*,
III, chapt. 28.[27] Many of the songs scattered through the text are

[24] Chambers, op. cit., II, 21–2.
[25] M. C. Bradbrook, *The Growth and Structure of Elizabethan Comedy*
(London, 1955), p. 47. A theme as well known to the diversified Blackfriars
audience as the prodigal son could be expected to trigger off varying comic
responses. Like Pantomime, it caters on one level to those who identify with
the characters, and on another to the more sophisticated, able to appreciate a
burlesque of the story's improbability, a parody of dramatic types and
language, and sallies of bawdry, wit, and political satire.
[26] H. D. Curtis, 'Source of the Petronel-Winifred Plot in "*Eastward Ho*" ',
MP, V (1907), 105–8.
[27] A. J. Farmer, 'Une Source de *Eastward Hoe*: Rabelais', *Études Anglaises*,
IV (1937), 325.

corruptions of popular airs by Dowland and Campion. Quicksilver's *Repentance* is modelled on Mannington's ballad written before his death in Cambridge (see below, Note V, v, 37, p. 110).

An alchemical shorthand almost certainly helped the three authors to unify their separate efforts. All the authors must have been familiar with ideas of alchemical transformation embodied in the plot. Any of the number of alchemical treatises with which Jonson was familiar (see H. & S., X, 46–7), may have provided the source for the interaction which had to occur before mercury was changed to gold.

THE PLAY

Eastward Ho! is a masterpiece of city comedy—a genre which presents London society in a realistic, satiric, and unsentimental light. The unity and cohesiveness with which the three authors combined their mature skills are such that in some respects they surpass the major comedies written independently.

> There is a geniality of spirit in *Eastward Hoe* foreign to Marston, a definition of character and a restraint in incident above Chapman, and a fluidity of movement and naturalness of manner not always to a similar degree Jonson's.[28]

But beyond its extraordinary success as a collaboration, *Eastward Ho!* deserves to be ranked among the greatest Jacobean comedies including Shakespeare's.

As Professor Bradbrook observes, the best Elizabethan comedy resides between 'two extremes of irony and sympathy' as 'in the plays of Shakespeare [where] the impulse towards identification and the impulse towards judgement might be simultaneously evoked'.[29] It is exactly this sagacious tone which makes *Eastward Ho!* unique among the 'coterie' city comedies written for boy players.[30] Citizens are not drawn with the sympathy shown in Dekker's celebration of bourgeois ideals, *The Shoemaker's Holiday*. Nor are they caricatured as gross and inept like the citizens of Beaumont's brilliant satire of citizen taste, *The Knight of the Burning Pestle*. *Eastward Ho!* goes further by presenting all classes in a mood of critical enjoyment which depends neither on sympathy for, nor antagonism against, any particular class. Critical realism distances the world of *Eastward Ho!* and allows a full satiric treatment simultaneously didactic, ironic, and triumphantly comic.

Two of the collaborators, Marston and Jonson, pioneered city comedy in the late 1590s and early 1600s, but it was not until 1604, when the bitterness of their 'stage quarrel' had been forgotten, that the two former opponents and Jonson's friend, Chapman, joined to

[28] F. E. Schelling, ed., *Eastward Hoe by Jonson, Chapman and Marston and Jonson's The Alchemist*. Belles-Lettres Series (Boston, 1903), p. xiii.
[29] Muriel C. Bradbrook, op. cit., p. 31.
[30] For a detailed description of the 'coterie' audience and their particular tastes see Alfred Harbage, *Shakespeare and the Rival Traditions* (N.Y., 1952).

write this genial comedy of London life. The catalyst may well have been *Westward Ho!*, a derivative city comedy by Dekker and Webster, produced by Paul's Boys late in 1604. It was probably Marston, a shareholder in the Queen's Revels, who commissioned Jonson and Chapman to help him challenge the success of the rival company.

In spite of the facetious tone with which the *Prologue* dismisses *Westward Ho!*, there can be little doubt that the founders of city comedy were nettled by the 'claptrap appeal'[31] and shoddy realism which had brought Dekker and Webster approval. They had copied the formula for city comedy from the Jonsonian model without Jonson's integrity or insight. London life is reproduced with sedulous attention to surface detail, but the effect is two-dimensional. The authors abandon satiric themes to relate a farcical cony-catching intrigue as fatuous as it is formless.

Eastward Ho! reveals the shallowness of its predecessor by exploiting the abandoned satiric themes and by parodying its form. It shows 'one thing that your cittizens wife coms short of to your Lady' (*Westward Ho!*, I, i, 26-7; ed. Bowers) and creates an atmosphere where 'Court, Citty and Countrey, are meerely as masks one to the other' (*Westward Ho!*, I, i, 227-8). The mood is also consciously critical of the posturing antics of such typical city comedy types as Petronel and Gertrude. Attitudes and language of typical city comedy are criticized in the debate between the prodigals and the prudent, in which both are satirized so that we see beneath the surface to the causes of social and artistic disorder. Jacobean vices have deep roots in the contemporary political and economic abuses; vice and virtue alike are deflated by burlesquing the way in which the characters adopt popular stage roles.[32]

The prologue of the play announces the theme, though in an extremely ambiguous way. It explains that the title honours 'the sun's rising', and this motto is connected throughout with the restless desire of the prodigals to leave behind the dull conventionality of the city for glory or gain. The new knight, Sir Petronel Flash, has already made the trip 'Eastward Ho!' where, according to the

---

[31] L. B. Wright, *Middle Class Culture in Elizabethan England* (Chapel Hill, 1935), p. 630.

[32] As Dr Brian Gibbons comments: 'By calling attention to their parody of crude dramatic realism Jonson, Chapman and Marston direct us to the real satiric concerns—both literary and social—which underlie the whole play, and reveal perhaps unexpectedly sophisticated possibilities in critical realism. We are given not literal accuracy of reporting, but intelligent dialectic'. Brian Gibbons, *Jacobean City Comedy. A Study of Satiric Plays by Jonson, Marston and Middleton* (London, 1968), p. 155.

gentleman of IV, i, 169–70, he 'stole his knighthood o'the grand day for four pound'. At best he is 'one of my thirty-pound knights' (IV, i, 168), a satirical portrait of the type of adventurer who flocked to London after the accession of James I (1603) to honour the sun's (king's) rising and to pursue 'Don Phoebus'—the prospect of easy gold.

In the first act of *Eastward Ho!* we see the shattering repercussions on the city of wholesale distribution of honours by the new king. As we join the play, Quicksilver is preparing to cast aside his apprenticeship to sail the Court seas—'Eastward Ho!'. The goldsmith's daughter, Gertrude, imagining herself a lady, wants to abandon the 'Bow-bell' in Cheapside for her 'knight's Eastward Castle'. Petronel, who is already up to his neck in debt, harnesses Quicksilver's dissatisfaction to extort Gertrude's land in order to finance the Virginian venture, a trip which must begin with a voyage eastward down the Thames, and might end in a land where even the chamber pots are gold. Finally, the tradesman, Touchstone, is rebuked by his wife for not sharing in the honours. She says of Petronel, 'he is a knight; and so might you have been, too, if you had been aught else than an ass, as well as some of your neighbours' (I, ii, 97–9).

But Touchstone is not tempted to rise above his class. He is a staunch believer in the bourgeois ethic, and quick to identify the pitfalls of opportunism. As he tells Quicksilver, 'Eastward Ho will make you go Westward Ho' (II, i, 112), and whereas the trip down the Thames to Greenwich is associated with adventure, the gallows of Tyburn at the western extremity is a grim warning of the fate which awaits those who attempt to overreach themselves at the expense of the city. Touchstone, a thoroughgoing citizen, has a vested interest in realizing his predictions against those whose sloth or pretensions threaten to upset the social order.

It is the usurer, Security, who benefits most from the rising ambitions of the prodigals. Whereas Touchstone tries to conciliate them to the routine of the city, Security exploits their sense of frustration for his own personal gain. He is unwilling to risk his money for the good of the city and lives off the more adventurous. Quicksilver summarizes the way in which Security's avarice fosters vice: 'Come, old Security, thou father of destruction . . . Thou feed'st my lechery, and I thy covetousness; thou art pander to me for my wench, and I to thee for thy cozenages' (II, ii, 10–15). With sardonic relish Security manipulates the unstable equilibrium to the detriment of society as a whole.

To Touchstone, the spokesman for medieval order, hard work, thrift, and honesty are the pillars which support the just society. For him, usury is 'the horn of suretyship . . . where the young fellow slips in at the butt-end, and comes squeezed out at the buckle' (I, i, 51–4). In alchemical terms he is trying to cure youth made base by the sulphur of acquisitiveness and the lead of false pride. He also sees it as his duty to mould the amenable into models of himself. It is, however, his simple faith in tradesmen's notions of alchemy and economics which makes him appear a quack(salver) rather than a prophet. Fate and a changed Golding redress the balance.

The play's alchemical-humour concepts necessitate a balanced structure of symmetrical oppositions. In the opening scene Touchstone and Quicksilver enter at opposite doors, while the industrious apprentice Golding, at the centre door, opens the business for trade. Touchstone, as his name indicates, sees himself as the 'Philosopher's Stone to make a golden temper', and takes it upon himself to convert the mercurial Quicksilver into a virtuous Golding. In character, situation, and dialogue this alchemical process is artificial. The artificiality is heightened by the 'prodigal son' motif, which further demands a special degree of stylized speech and movement; all apparently earnest in manner, so that the characters' behaviour, though realistic, tends towards allegory. The boy actors are deliberately shown at some distance from normal behaviour in order that the spectator can freely laugh across the gap. Thus in the first scene Golding's symbolic tripping-up of the prodigal is seen in both real and allegorical terms ('GOLDING *trips up* [QUICKSILVER's] *heels and holds him*'; s.d. following I, i, 126). This action temporarily restores the balance by good-naturedly showing an ounce of gold equal to a bushel of 'feathers' (nonsense).

The same kind of imbalance which exists between master and apprentice pits the wanton daughter Gertrude against her father. Gertrude's sanguine attitude to lovemaking reveals her as a delightful caricature of the lusty citizen seeking rank, while her sister Mildred is blandly conventional and sober. Touchstone wants 'to prove' in Mildred's marriage that 'mean' love is superior to 'lofty love' (I, ii, 164–5), whilst Mistress Touchstone, who encourages Gertrude's haughty pretensions, will prove the opposite. Thus, though the Touchstones identify impurities in the 'metal' as in the 'humour' characters, they also excite them: they are themselves governed by the same kind of all-pervading inclination. As Touchstone says: 'My wife has her humour, and I will ha' mine' (I, ii, 144–5).

The role of the Touchstones is to reveal humours, not to cure them, and their efforts to become philosophers (stones) are ludicrous. The Touchstones' aim to cure the prodigals of their humours is undermined by the sinister usurer, the melancholic Security. Security's 'hunger and thirst', like Volpone's, is a sensuous manifestation of his economic vice. He hoards gold in his 'cave', feeds the humours of would-be gallants like Quicksilver, and cheats knights and citizens of all they possess. It is, however, his very classic humour of 'stern usurous jealousy' (III, ii, 257) which foreshadows his own self-gulling and breakdown into suspicion, doubt, and desperation. His pathetic song bewailing his saturnine state (V, v, 133–40) is not, as Herford thinks, out of character.[33]

Where Touchstone's warnings fail to effect any change, the 'red tempest' and tide on the Thames succeed. The appearance of Slitgut, a curiously godlike commentator, heightens the intended allegory in the Cuckold's Haven scene.[34] The upstarts, who drunkenly embark eastward from Billingsgate (the first leg of their trip to Mammon's paradise, Virginia), are driven back by tide and tempest, and robbed of their ill-gotten gains by the 'greedy Thames' which rudely casts them up at the stations of their humours.

Security, the villain of the piece, who has unknowingly pandered his wife to Petronel, is washed up at Cuckold's Haven. He is so broken in spirit that he exits like the vanquished Morality Play Satan, creeping 'on the earth' (IV, i, 49). His wife, the would-be whore, appropriately lands in disarray at the site of the nunnery of Saint Katherine's. Meanwhile Sir Petronel is cast up on the Isle of Dogs hard by the Palace of Greenwich to be dubbed 'he that stole his knighthood . . . for four pound' (IV, i, 169–70) by passing gentry.[35] Finally, the ostentatious Quicksilver is delivered, '*bareheaded*', before the ominous gallows at Wapping. The prevailing winds of Fortune have pushed the miscreants Eastward Ho!, but rather than bring them riches it has reduced them to their humours. The fate of the villains is mocked by the horned god at Cuckold's Haven—a revenge for the insults and greed they have inflicted upon the city.

'Eastward Ho!', as Touchstone predicts, now leads 'Westward Ho!' Gertrude, duped out of her inheritance through her own vanity, rides east to find her castle 'made of air', and returns by Weeping

---

[33] H. & S., II, 42. Security's pessimism after the storm is as alchemically predictable as Quicksilver's hasty recovery.

[34] The character of Slitgut is indeed strange, for though a butcher's apprentice, he has the insight of an astrologer, or a god. His name is appropriate in that gluttony and greed are the outward manifestation of the malefactor's *hubris*. (See II, i, 39–48 where Touchstone complains of the City's gluttony; Security's catch phrase, 'how I do hunger and thirst to do you good'; and Petronel's remarks about the drunkenness before the storm.) Slitgut is the City's chorus for the comic humiliation of the City's enemies. The storm is thus a direct result of a breach in degree by the upstarts.

[35] See *Date and Sources* (above, p. xxiii). The association of royalty with this spot may also derive from the occasion when Queen Elizabeth knighted Sir Francis Drake at Greenwich.

Cross (IV, ii, 22). The victims of the storm return unrepentant to the city to be further humiliated by Touchstone's fiery wrath and cast into the Counter. But if Fate (the City) frustrates ambitions founded on greed, it rewards Golding, who 'stands and waits', by raising him to the position of alderman.

At last a man of virtue is in the pivotal position and order can be restored. The city's equilibrium, upset by the self-seekers, is re-established by three of Golding's gentlemanly actions: firstly, he sends gold to restore Quicksilver's spirit; secondly, he tricks Touchstone into witnessing the Repentance; and thirdly, to cap it all, he suggests that Security should pay Sindefy's dowry. For this he wins a plaudit as a gentleman, and he deserves to be congratulated. Golding arbitrates a compromise between the adventurers and the citizens, ensuring that the general prosperity (a by-product of fortune-seeking) is not arrested by usurious avarice or inhibited by bourgeois probity. The play's dedication to the City, though ambiguous, is not totally facetious. Fate favours those who keep things running smoothly and punishes those who upset the equilibrium.

An alchemical shorthand almost certainly helped the three authors to present the characters in their economic humours. The names 'Touchstone', 'Quicksilver', and 'Golding' predict their attitudes and actions. Colours play an allegorical role in revealing changes in character. The notion of alchemical change informs the Cuckold's Haven scene where the 'red tempest' gives the malefactors a ritual washing in the Thames, and they are 'alchemically' initiated. In the next scene Golding appears dressed in red, the colour of philosopher's gold, and through his intervention Quicksilver (the infected mercury) is converted. In the final scene Security, who wears the colour of his vice, jealousy—sulphurous yellow—is left as a pathetic caricature of his saturnine nature.

Instead of ignoring class conflicts, *Eastward Ho!* emphasizes tensions to create a world of instability in which Fate is the controlling hand and irony the comic vision. The decorum of the 'prodigal son' opening scenes is superseded by comic anarchy, culminating in the Cuckold's Haven catastrophe. When the parable is reasserted gratuitously in the final acts the effect is ironic rather than didactic. The last scene is a brilliant parody of the morality play conclusion. Touchstone's thumping moral is an obvious poke at plays like *Liberality and Prodigality* (1601; Blackfriars) and *The London Prodigal* (c. 1604; Globe).

By Jonson's definition comedy is concerned with the representation of the ridiculous. His comment, like most Elizabethan treatises on the nature of comedy, recalls Aristotle's definition in the fifth chapter of the *Poetics*. Here comedy is described as 'an imitation of men

· ·

worse than the average; worse, however, not as regards every sort of fault, but only as regards one particular kind, the Ridiculous, which is a species of the Ugly'.[36] The definitive statement on the ridiculous comes from Henry Fielding's preface to *Joseph Andrews*: 'the only source of the true ridiculous [is] affectation, [and this] proceeds from two causes, vanity and hypocrisy'.[37] Fielding, himself a master of comic incongruity and Ridiculous surprise, acknowledges Jonson as a master of the risible, and his ideas become important in a consideration of the comic method of *Eastward Ho!*

The play's theme of intransigence and mutability is made vigorous by a clever use of double-edged satire. Vanity and hypocrisy are shown as the extremes of ridiculousness; once they are exposed comic decorum triumphs. The conceit and licentiousness of Gertrude and Quicksilver make them the willing victims of Sir Petronel's assumed rank and Security's greed. The two arch-hypocrites gull each other of their most prized possessions—Petronel loses his wife's land but gains Winifred, Security's wife. In the Cuckold's Haven scene each is made to recognize his folly, and, though they temporarily revert, capture, reprimand, and imprisonment force them to contemplate their guilt and repent.

But if satire cuts one way to reveal acquisitiveness disguised as vanity, it also exposes the demure complacence and bourgeois propriety of Golding and Mildred for what it is. Both are wooden Puritans so preoccupied with their homilies of thrift and modesty as to seem pusillanimous. Thus whereas the prodigals are forced to realize the error of their ways, their foils become targets for those with less money and more wit. As Anthony Caputi observes, 'the explicit norms of behaviour established by Touchstone, Golding and Mildred . . . are as comic [ridiculous] as the deviations from them'.[38]

Even Touchstone, whose virtue and honesty stand in contrast to Security's vice and hypocrisy, is treated indulgently. As Caputi says, 'he is an honest tradesman the way the fashionable audience at Blackfriars conceived of such honest tradesmen—with his tagline: "Work upon that now", and his "good wholesome thrifty sentences"...' His 'self-righteousness' and 'vindictiveness' when he learns that the prodigals are at his mercy, and his 'sentimentality and gullibility' when shown a reformed Quicksilver, all mark him as a man who

[36] Aristotle, *Poetics*, 5. M. T. Herrick, *Comic Theory in The Sixteenth Century* (Urbana, Illinois, 1950), p. 38.
[37] Henry Fielding, 'Preface', *Joseph Andrews*, The Works of Henry Fielding in 11 vols., ed. J. Browne, V (London, 1903), 15.
[38] Anthony Caputi, op. cit., p. 226. [Their virtue is as pompous as the rogues' pretended virtue is incongruous.]

takes his tradesman's dignity too seriously.[39] His belief in miraculous conversion is, if not ridiculous, childishly naïve. Thus the badinage of citizen propriety, unmalicious though it is, counterpoints the deeper satire of fraud and deception.

If the aim of Jonsonian comedy is to expose the ridiculous to laughter, *Eastward Ho!* is in the best traditions of this comedy. It certainly follows Fielding's description of Jonson's comic practice:

> From the discovery of this affectation arises the Ridiculous . . . and that in a higher and stronger degree when affectation arises from hypocrisy, than when from vanity: for to discover any one to be exact the reverse of what he affects, is more surprising, and consequently more ridiculous, than to find him a little deficient in the quality he desires the reputation of.[40]

In the last three acts we witness the affectations of Gertrude, Quicksilver, and Sir Petronel exposed as folly and the insidious hypocrite, Security, gulled and humiliated. Satire is thus used to deflate pretensions and to show the self-defeating nature of greed; while the 'deficient' bourgeois types by their sheer lack of vitality touch on caricature. But the response is less a scorn for the crimes of the transgressors than delight in 'an Image of the times'.[41] It fulfils Jonson's injunction (and Horace's) that comedy should 'both delight and teach'.[42] The predictability of the prodigal son types allows for burlesque, but this is not so flagrant or sardonic as in other coterie plays.[43] Rather, the mood is one of facetious delight in which affectation and folly are ridiculed and enjoyed wherever they are found and virtue is rewarded with patronizing good humour.

The world of *Eastward Ho!* is given perspective by a critical

---

[39] ibid., p. 225.

[40] Henry Fielding, op. cit., 16.

[41] Ben Jonson, 1616 Folio Prologue, 23, *Every Man In His Humour*, H. & S., III, 303.

[42] Jonson, 'Discoveries', H. & S., VIII, 643.

[43] Dr Andrew Gurr in a recent book, *The Shakespearean Theatre 1574–1642* (Cambridge, 1970), p. 144, refutes Harbage's theory that *Knight of the Burning Pestle* (1607) failed because its attack on the citizens 'lacked animus'. Professor Gurr writes, 'it is also worth bearing in mind that the first performance of Beaumont's *Knight of the Burning Pestle* at the Blackfriars in 1607 was a flop because, as the publisher of the first quarto (1613) said, the audience missed "the privie mark of irony about it". That a burlesque of citizen plays should be construed by the audience as a straight citizen play rather implies that the citizen element in the audience was stronger than Beaumont bargained for'. If *Knight of the Burning Pestle* failed because it exploited divisions in the audience too far, would it not be plausible that *Eastward Ho!* succeeded because it reconciled them?

dialectic so that it never sinks into sentimentality or hardens to cynicism, and the ridiculous is criticized and purged before comic order is restored. Between the two extremes of ridiculousness a 'mean' is implied which suggests the norm of 'the gentlemanly point of view'.

Since Professor Harbage's study in *Shakespeare and the Rival Traditions* there has been much debate in academic circles about the composition of the audience in the private theatres. The most recent studies have modified the idea that the audience was a class-conscious coterie. Thornberry's dissertation *Shakespeare and the Blackfriars Tradition 1600–06* concluded that

> in play after play, the Blackfriars dramatists exerted considerable effort to convey the standards of the 'gentlemanly' sector of society and to prevent the clan from being debased, and they did so by establishing the norm and satirizing both those who deviate from it and those who try to rise into the group from below.[44]

The debate between Quicksilver and Touchstone implies just this norm. Quicksilver emulates the 'gentlemen of good phrase, perfect language, passingly behaved; gallants that wear socks and clean linen' (I, i, 59–61), though he is an apprentice; whereas Touchstone explains that thrift and hard work are more important than 'gallants' company' (I, i, 45). Similarly Gertrude believes herself 'fit to be a lady' (V, i, 121), and Mildred says 'I judge them truly mad that yoke citizens and courtiers' (I, ii, 38–9). True gentlemen, well-educated gallants of the Inns of Court of the type believed to have frequented the Blackfriars, do appear, only to snub Sir Petronel (IV, i, 156–72).

The ridiculous way in which the upstarts ape gentlemanly conduct is heightened by burlesque of the heroes of the popular (adult) stage. This type of parody was ideally suited to the boys' supposed style of acting, and to an audience intellectually aware of literary pursuits. Petronel's entrance '*in boots, with a riding wand*' makes fun of the laboured realism of such conventional city comedies as *Westward Ho!*

PETRONEL
I'll out of this wicked town as fast as my horse can trot. Here's now no good action for a man to spend his time in. Taverns grow dead; ordinaries are blown up; plays are at a stand; houses of hospitality at a fall; not a feather waving, nor a spur jingling anywhere. (II, iii, 1–5)

Or imagine the effect on the gentlemen of a boy grotesquely imitating the stylized tripping of a lady (I, ii, 58–64). As with the debate based on the exchange of 'gold ends' for 'play ends' (prosaic proverbs for

[44] R. Thornberry, *Shakespeare and the Blackfriars Tradition* (*1600–06*). Unpublished PhD thesis, Ohio State University (1964), p. 67.

tragic rant), the satire is directed not only at characters but also at the exploitation of such types for stage purposes. When Touchstone anticipates the presentation of Golding's deeds on the popular stage, or Gertrude reflects on the former glories of knighthood, we have examples of the mocking of sentimental romantic comedy.

Parody and witty dialogue rich in puns and bawdry cater to a sophisticated audience critically aware of style. *Eastward Ho!* is no insipid morality play. A search for the true gold of aristocratic virtue ends in marriage, the symbol of alchemical transformation. But this is the marriage of an upstart gentleman to a whore whose dowry is paid by a usurer, and it is proclaimed a victory for the citizen, Touchstone. In fact both apprentices learn to respect the social order: Quicksilver has learnt not 'to go beyond his tether' while Golding wins a plaudit as a true gentleman for magnanimity in helping his peer Quicksilver. A moral is illustrated, but there is no serious attempt at edification. Because Quicksilver's repentance is more expedient than sincere, Touchstone's victory is hollow: Fate is the true arbiter of the City's fortune. If, as the *Prologue* indicates, the title is not entirely 'enforced', then neither is the dedication to the City. The play reveals the usurer, not the citizen or gallant, as the true enemy of City, Court, and Country. *Eastward Ho!*, though it honours the spirit of adventure, is dedicated to the tradesmen who pay the bills.

STAGE HISTORY

According to the title page of *Eastward Ho!* it was first acted by the 'Children of Her Majesties Revels', at the Blackfriars in 1605. The imprisonment of the authors seems to have made the play a *succès de scandale* when it first appeared and a voracious reading public demanded three editions before the end of 1605. In spite of the king's initial anger with the Scots satire, it was played again by Lady Elizabeth's Men (former Queen's Revels) in the summer of 1613 and on 25 January 1614 at Court.

In 1685 Nahum Tate presented a three-act farce entitled *Cuckold's Haven, or an Alderman no Conjuror* at the Dorset Garden theatre. This badly bowdlerized version catered to Restoration tastes for foppery and foolery.

It was twice revived in the eighteenth century: first unsuccessfully by Garrick, who substituted it for a far more brazen comedy of manners (Ravenscroft's *The London Cuckolds*) on 29 October 1751. In 1775 Charlotte Lennox wrote a successful adaptation following Garrick's suggestions and it was performed at Drury Lane under the title *Old City Manners*. She modernized Dodsley's (1744) text by cutting the parody of Hamlet; she added a jilted lover for Gertrude, and made Sir Petronel a disguised thief already married to a barmaid. Hogarth's famous series of drawings *Industry and Idleness* (1747) had, according to the Prologue, inspired her likewise to put the theme of *Eastward Ho!* in a contemporary setting.

The play has been revived at various schools and universities throughout this century; and Wren writes that he directed a successful production at Harpur College in 1960.[45] It was revived professionally in 1962 across the street from the site of its original production at The Mermaid Theatre, Puddle Dock. Directed by Josephine Wilson and Denys Palmer, this revival drew wide acclaim for its energy, though the *Guardian* reviewer thought there was a 'sacrifice of all subtlety to high spirits, headlong pace, and some sadly misplaced slapstick grimacing'. It struck the *Daily Telegraph* critic as an early 'Christmas show' and in the same vein *The Times* called it a 'local pageant' acted in a style resembling 'the straight passages in a Christmas Pantomime'. Kenneth Tynan (the *Observer*) was impressed by the 'earthiness of the class satire' and praised the play as 'among the funniest of its kind'. He thought the production 'a model of organised exuberance'.

[45] See Wren, op. cit., pp. 340–4.

NOTE ON THE TEXT

Eastward Ho! was entered in the Stationers' Register by William Aspley and Thomas Thorpe on 4 September 1605. Three quartos followed, all with similar type ornaments (George Eld's)[46] and the 1605 imprint. The first quarto (hereafter Qq) collates A–I⁴ and is found in two issues, a^i and a^{ii}. In the latter, two leaves, E3 and E4, were cancelled and replaced by a reset cancellans. The following seven and a half lines, evidently those offensive to King James and his Scots entourage, were thus removed from the text:

> . . . onely a few industrious Scots perhaps, who indeed are disperst ouer the face of the whole earth. But as for them, there are no greater friends to English men and *England*, when they are out an't, in the world, then they are. And for my part, I would a hundred thousand of 'hem were there, for wee are all one Countreymen now, yee know; and wee should finde ten time more comfort of them there, then wee doe heere.   (III, iii, 38–45)

Furthermore, the statement that in Virginia 'you may be a Noble man, and neuer be a Slaue' has been altered to 'you may be any other officer, and neuer be a Slaue' in a^{ii}. To disguise the cancel, three lines were added at III, iii, 51:

> . . . Besides, there, we shall haue no more Law then Conscience, and not too much of either; serue God inough, eate and drinke inough, and *inough is as good as a Feast.*

Ashley 371, the former Wise copy now in the British Museum, is the only known copy of the uncancelled issue, a^i, but even this is imperfect. A note on its end-paper confirms that 'the title A1 is supplied from a copy of another [a third] edition, now at Texas', though 'a photocopy of the title originally belonging to this copy . . . is inserted. . . .'[47] The Victoria and Albert Museum's copy (a^{ii}) preserves the only other known example of the cancellandum E3 ^{r}–E4 ^{v}.

---

[46] H. & S., IV, 490.

[47] Thomas Wise, who has become notorious for his fraudulent practices, stupidly switched these pages to increase the value of his first edition. He thus 'mutilated a unique copy'. See D. F. Foxon, *Thomas J. Wise and Pre-Restoration Drama. A Study in Theft and Sophistication.* London, *Supplement to the Bibliographical Publications*, 19 (1959), pp. 6, 38.

The second and third quartos, b and c, derive directly from a^{ii}, correcting a few obvious errors and amplifying others. Both quartos save one sheet by increasing the number of lines per page and by adopting a number of abbreviations (i.e., they collate A–H^4). b has the same title-page as Qq and its last sheet incorporates standing type from a^{ii}.[48] It must, therefore, have followed hard on the heels of the first quarto. The third quarto has a rearranged title-page, but reproduces the second more or less page for page. As b and c are derivative texts, and the a^{ii} cancellans appears to be a compelled change rather than the authors' intention to improve upon the original, I believe the cancellandum version, Ashley 371, to be the most authoritative text. For this reason it was chosen as the copy text for this edition (hereafter Q).

From Q it appears that the printer's copy was probably authorial foul papers or a scribe's fair copy of them (see above, *Authorship*, p. xviii). The confusion between the character names *Spendall* and *Spoyl*. (III, i, 52, 61), the appearance of the near-ghost character, Bettrice (I, ii, 1 s.d.), and the lack of adequate stage directions for Gertrude's departure (III, ii, 182), for the storm scene (IV, i), and for the episodes in the Counter (V, iii–v), all witness the characteristic vagueness of foul papers. No prompter, however careless, would leave unmarked one entrance and eleven exits; nor would he fail to complete the three stage directions and two songs ending in 'etc.'. Illegible or carelessly revised copy might also explain the two consecutive speeches given *2 Pris.* (V, v, 10), why Slitgut's last speech is unassigned (IV, i, 268), and the four misplaced and four redundant stage directions.

Eleven of the thirteen existing copies of the first quarto were collated for this edition. These were: Ashley 371 and C56 d32 from the British Museum; the Dyce copy from the Victoria and Albert Museum; Mal. 765 and Mal. 252, the Bodleian and Worcester College copies, respectively; and copies from the Yale, Folger, Massachusetts Institute of Technology, Huntington, Clark, and Pforzheimer libraries in America. Unfortunately I was unable to consult the copies belonging to the Boston Public Library and the Library of Congress.

The collation of Qq revealed only five substantive corrections, all of which have little textual significance.[49] There were 114 accidentals excluding the 95 variants created when $E3^r$–$E4^v$ was reset. Only five formes were without minor variants—A inner, C outer, H inner and outer, and I outer, while the others showed a multitude

---

[48] H. & S., IV, 501–2.
[49] See below, Appendix 4; Press Corrections.

of corrections to spelling and punctuation. The mass of accidentals might be due to the state of the foul papers from which Qq was set, but they could also have arisen if the preliminary proofing was more concerned with censorship than with weeding out minor errors.

From earlier studies of Eld's printing, we know that his shop had two presses and employed at least four workmen. The picture established by Alice Walker, Akihiro Yamada, and G. B. Evans[50] of Eld A and Eld B, active 1605–09, suggests that the two men responsible for setting *Eastward Ho!* can be identified by the following characteristic spelling preferences.

Eld A	*Eld B*
'els' 'shalbe'	'else' 'shall be' (Walker)
'y' endings	'ie' endings (Yamada, Evans)
'e' in 'me', 'he', etc.	'ee' in 'mee', 'hee', etc.
	(Yamada, Evans)

In addition, the following distinctive spellings are almost invariably characteristic:

careless setting of verse	careless setting of speech
'can't punctuate intelligibly' (Walker)	prefixes
'Ahlas' 'bene' 'lets' 'blood'	'Alas' 'bin' 'let's' 'bloud'
'forth' 'i'faith' 'hart'	'foorth' 'y'faith' 'heart'
'cannot' *'Mist. Touch.'*	'can not' *'Mistris Touch.'*
'd' = ed in 'praisd', etc.	' 'd' = ed in 'prais'd', etc.
'a' in 'change', etc.	'au' in 'chaunge', etc.
'i' in 'voice', etc.	'y' in 'voyce', etc.
'g' in 'voyage', etc.	'dge' in 'voyadge', etc.
'Wolfe.'	*'Woolfe.'*

An analysis of the text on the basis of these spelling preferences produces this enigmatic compositorial pattern.

Eld A appears to have set: A2^v?, A3^v–A4^r?; B2^v–B4^r?; D1^v–D4^r; E2^v–E4^r?; F1^r–F1^v?, F4^r–H2^r; H4^v; I2^v–I4^r. = 37 pages. Eld B probably set: A1^v–A2^r?, A3^r?, A4^v?–B2^r; B4^v–D1^r; D4^v–E2^r, E4^v; F2^r–F3^v; H2^v–H4^r; I1^r–I2^r, I4^v; and probably reset E3^r–E4^v? = 34 pages and 4 resets.

[50] See: Alice Walker, ed., New Cambridge *Troilus and Cressida*, pp. 122–34; A. Yamada, 'Bibliographical Studies of George Chapman's *All Fools* (1605); Printed by George Eld', *The Shakespeare Society of Japan*, III (1964), 73–99; and G. B. Evans, 'Textual Introduction', *All Fools. The Plays of George Chapman: The Comedies, A Critical Edition*, gen. ed. Alan Holaday (Urbana, Ill., 1971), pp. 227–32. (My Eld A is Walker's Eld A, Yamada's Eld D, and Evans's Eld C; while Eld B is so called in all three earlier studies.)

In the proposed assignment, those stints followed by a '?' are open to argument, while the others are ascribed confidently.

Eld A, as in *Troilus and Cressida*, is the faster of the two compositors, and the less accurate in punctuation. The pattern of setting in B, E, H, I is similar to that of sheet K in the later play. It is also noteworthy that Eld B's stint B4^v–D1^r corresponds exactly to Chapman's first segment (see above, *Authorship*, p. xvi), and that Eld A's long passage F4^r–H2^r was almost certainly the first passage written entirely by Jonson. The independent setting of these two passages corresponds with the notion that *Eastward Ho!* was set from foul papers, since it would be far easier for each compositor to work individually with the work of one author, especially if they worked from cast-off copy, as it appears they did.

The pattern of running titles does not correspond to the compositorial division. Three sets of running titles (4 in each set) were employed in the printing of *Eastward Ho!*: 1 for inner and outer A, C, F, and outer I; 2 for inner and outer B, D, G, and inner I; and 3 for inner and outer E and H. It may be significant that the introduction of set 3 corresponds with a more frequent recurrence of broken letters after E. This might suggest that after E there was a greater rate of distribution, because the press was held up by proofing of the early gatherings.

Professor J. Quincy Adams and C. H. Herford came to the independent conclusion that even Q does not represent the play 'As it was Playd in the *Black-friers*'. The circumstantial evidence that certain pages with fewer than the average number of type lines allude to the Court prompted Adams's hypothesis that, after the trouble arising from performance, the 'wary' publisher must have revised these pages in proof before printing.[51] Herford does not conjecture on what persuaded the printer to make his belated attempts to clear the text of dangerous matter, but he does reproduce type facsimiles of these pages in *Ben Jonson*, IV, 508–14. Adams estimates that about 29 lines were cut, Herford only 17;[52] but neither considers the nature of the printer's copy or the compositorial vicissitudes.

Unfortunately, circumstantial evidence is not enough to prove that the shortened pages witness the hurried revision of the text by the printer. The wide slugs around the unnecessarily double-spaced stage directions on A3^r suggest the possibility of a rearrangement at I, i, 76, but could also have resulted from a misestimation in casting off. On A4^v the printing of I, ii, 48–50 as verse rather than

[51] J. Q. Adams, op. cit., 157–69.
[52] ibid.: 4 or 5 from A3^r, 8 from A4^v, 6 from C1^v, 5 from C2^r, and 5 from E4^r. H. & S., IV, 495–9: 9 from A4^v, 4 from C1^v, 4 from C2^r, and signs of revision on A3^r, B1^v–B2^r, and E3^v–E4^r.

prose might evidence the printer's efforts to expand the existing text to fill the space left by the removal of lines; it might also be the compositor's misreading of verse, or his compensation for faulty casting off. The gap (III, iii, 58) on the original E4^r, similarly, could be accounted for by the missetting of verse at III, ii, 275–84, 289–290, and 312–24, rather than by the removal of satire.[53] The strongest argument in favour of the revision theory is the spacing of C1^v–C2^r, two consecutive pages set by the same compositor. These pages have 37 and 35 lines respectively, in contrast with the usual 39, and the central topic is the affairs of the Court. A gibe may well have been removed at II, ii, 80.

It is therefore conceivable that after setting and before presswork the text was revised. The impending publication of the play may have triggered the king's anger (see above, *Date and Sources*, pp. xxiv–xxv). In order to avoid implication, the publisher might have had type removed from A3^r, A4^v, C1^v, and C2^r (in all, about 14 lines could have been struck in this way), while the incriminating satire of E3^v–E4^r could have escaped notice until shortly after the first issue went on sale. The cancel might then be seen as the printer's last effort to clear the text of dangerous material.

Only one other flaw has been attributed to Q. Chambers supposes Slitgut's last speech was misplaced, suggesting that it be moved to IV, i, 230 so that a new scene can open when Winifred and the Drawer enter 'before the Blue Anchor Tavern, Billingsgate'.[54] Simpson takes this point in *Ben Jonson*, IX, 644, 665, although it was by then too late for him to alter his original ordering (Q's) of the text. But the specific references to time in the text, and the thematic coherence of the scene in its present form, argue for the quarto's order. Chambers clearly misinterprets Winifred's 'taking bed' in St Katherine's as an overnight stay, when in fact she lands there in the early morning (IV, i, 6), and stays only until the Drawer can fetch her clothes from the Blue Anchor (IV, i, 89–91)—no great length of time. Her ploy depends on close secrecy from the friendly Drawer, and a quick return to the city. The passage of time between her rescue at St Katherine's and her reappearance 'near' (not, as Chambers would have it, 'before') the Blue Anchor, is indicated by the intervening action, particularly in Quicksilver's apparent recovery of spirit between his despair when he lands at Wapping and his self-possession when he meets the other survivors on the Isle of Dogs (IV, i, 175–230). Thus, it is later *that* morning when Winifred comes

[53] I regard it as extremely unlikely that E3^v–E4^r was revised in the original. Would any publisher worried about satire leave such an obvious gird against the Scots as III, iii, 38–45?

[54] Chambers, op. cit., III, 149–50 and 150n.

upon Security; his dishevelled 'rags' confirm that her deception will succeed, while he is almost speechless to find her unscathed. She makes good her advantage by accusing him of stealing her clothes and staying 'all night abroad at taverns' (IV, i, 246–7). Winifred's 'new attire' and her story that she has waited all night 'patient and hopeful' totally convince Security of her innocence, so much so that he begins to doubt his previous sanity.

Whether Slitgut can observe this scene or not, Security's repentance for his 'jealousy and suspicion' make an appropriate moment for the 'red tempest's anger' to abate, and for Slitgut to descend 'his honourable prospect'. His panegyric to the piquant 'horn of destiny' thus beautifully rounds off a sequence in which poetic justice and more particularly cuckoldry triumph.

The Q has been followed faithfully, except when obvious compositorial mistakes were corrected in Qq or in the second quarto (B.M. 644 d53), which was also consulted. Spellings and punctuation have been modernized in keeping with present grammatical practice, except where alteration of Q would detract from dramatic characterization—i.e., many of Gertrude's affected pronunciations and her breathless run-on sentences were not altered. Q's speech rhythms and the fluidity of the prose have been maintained as far as possible. More editorial corrections have been made to Eld A's punctuation than to Eld B's. Like Herford I change III, ii, 275–84, 289–90, and 312–24 from prose to verse (Eld A's E2ᵛ–E3ʳ). But I see little justification in changing III, ii, 197–204, since it probably belongs to the more accurate Eld B.

The *Dramatis Personae*, scene locations, and stage directions follow C. F. Brooke and N. Paradise, eds., *Eastward Ho!* in *English Drama 1580–1612*, pp. 397–435. In addition I have moved the stage directions at IV, ii, 32, 157, 160 and in V, v, 24, which are squeezed into the wrong position in Q. The speech prefix for Slitgut's last speech is also forgotten in Qq (except in Dyce where it is written in). Like all editors after Dodsley I correct the obviously misassigned s.p. at V, v, 10 and give the *Epilogue* to Quicksilver. Unlike previous editors, I have inserted a stage direction for the monkey at I, ii, 46 to remind the reader of the possible revision of Q at this point. Other possible revisions are recorded in the notes.

Otherwise I follow the usual editorial conventions of this series: standardizing elisions; centring stage directions and not printing their final full stop; and removing unnecessary capitals and italics. I have changed the Latin act and scene divisions which occur in Qq to their English equivalents. All editorial emendations are denoted by square brackets, and silent corrections are recorded above the line at the bottom of the page.

CHART 1

The Number of Printed Lines Per Page

	1^r	1^v	2^r	2^v	3^r	3^v	4^r	4^v
A	—	—	35	37	*37*	39	38	*35*
B	39	38	39	36	39	39	39	39
C	39	*37*	*35*	39	39	38	39	39
D	39	35	39	34	38	39	38	39
E	39	39	39	39	38	*38*	*35*	39
F	39	39	36	38	39	40	39	39
G	39	40	40	39	39	39	39	39
H	39	39	40	40	40	39	39	39
I	39	39	40	40	40	38	36	41

Broken Letters Recurrence

Swash A A1^v, 12, G1^r, 2
Swash T A1^v, 11, D3^v, 6
Swash A A2^r, 3, D3^r, 37, F4^r, 17
Roman G A3^r, 27, E1^r, 15, F3^r, 21
Roman a A3^r, 24, E1^r, 18, I4^v, 12?
Swash T B1^v, 38, G1^v, 30
Roman h B4^v, 10, E1^v, 19
Roman h D2^r, 21, F1^v, 2

i.e., Inner forme of A had been distributed when D was being composed.

— Outer forme of A had been distributed when E was being composed.

— B had been distributed when E was being composed.

— D had been distributed when F was being composed.

Cancellation of E3^r–E4^r (reset) took place after the type for E had been distributed.

CHART 2

Running Titles

Styles Key: *EASTWARD HOE*   1

* = swash   *EASTWÅRD HOE*   2

                         EASTWÅR̊D HOE   3

                         EASTWAR̊D HOE   4

                         EÅSTWAR̊D HOE   5

                         EÅSTWÅRD HOE   6

                         EÅSTWARD HOE   7

Pattern

Inner Formes

A1^v – B1^v 1 C1^v 2 D1^v 1 E1^v 2 F1^v 2 G1^v 1 H1^v 2 I1^v 1

A2^r – B2^r 2 C2^r 3 D2^r 2 E2^r 7 F2^r 3 G2^r 2 H2^r 7 I2^r 2 *Reset*

A3^v 2 B3^v 5 C3^v 3 D3^v 5 E3^v 1 F3^v 3 G3^v 5 H3^v 1 I3^v 5 E3^v 3

A4^r 1 B4^r 4 C4^r 1 D4^r 4 E4^r 2 F4^r 1 G4^r 4 H4^r 2 I4^r 4 E4^r 4

Outer Formes

A1^r – B1^r 2 C1^r 3 D1^r 2 E1^r 6 F1^r 3 G1^r 2 H1^r 7 I1^r 3

A2^v 2 B2^v 1 C2^v 2 D2^v 1 E2^v 2 F2^v 2 G2^v 1 H2^v 2 I2^v 2

A3^r 1 B3^r 4 C3^r 1 D3^r 4 E3^r 2 F3^r 1 G3^r 4 H3^r 2 I3^r 1 E3^r 2

A4^v 3 B4^v 5 C4^v 3 D4^v 5 E4^v 1 F4^v 3 G4^v 5 H4^v 1 I4^v 3 E4^v 1

Conclusion: It appears that three sets of head titles were used. One set for inner and outer A, C, F, and I outer; a second for inner and outer B, D, G, and I inner; and a third for inner and outer E and H.

FURTHER READING

Adams, J. Q., 'Eastward Hoe and its Satire Against the Scots', *SP*, XXVIII (1931), 157–69.

Bradbrook, Muriel C., *The Growth and Structure of Elizabethan Comedy*, London, 1955 (reprinted, 1962).

Brettle, R. E., '*Eastward Ho*, 1605; by Chapman, Jonson, and Marston; Bibliography and Circumstances of Production', *The Library*, 4th Series, IX (1928–29), 287–302.

Caputi, Anthony, *John Marston Satirist*, N.Y., 1961.

Gibbons, Brian, *Jacobean City Comedy. A Study of Satire in Plays by Jonson, Marston and Middleton*, London, 1968.

Gurr, Andrew, *The Shakespearean Theatre 1574–1642*, Cambridge, 1970.

Harbage, Alfred, *Shakespeare and the Rival Traditions*, N.Y., 1952.

Herford, C. H., and Percy & Evelyn Simpson, eds., *Ben Jonson*, Oxford, 1925–52.

Holmyard, E. J., *Alchemy*, London, 1968.

Jacquot, Jean, *George Chapman, 1559–1634, sa vie, sa poésie, son théâtre, sa pensée*, Paris, 1951.

Judges, A. V., ed., *The Elizabethan Underworld: A Collection of Early Stuart Tracts and Ballads*, London, 1930 (reprinted, 1965).

Knights, L. C., *Drama and Society in the Age of Jonson*, London, 1962.

Parrott, T. M., ed., *The Plays and Poems of George Chapman*, 3 vols., *The Comedies*, II, London, 1913 (reissued N.Y., 1961).

Schoenbaum, Samuel, *Internal Evidence and Elizabethan Dramatic Authorship*, London, 1966.

Thornberry, Richard T., *Shakespeare and the Blackfriars Tradition (1600–06)*, unpublished PhD thesis, Ohio State University, 1964.

Tilley, M. P., *A Dictionary of Proverbs in England in the Sixteenth and Seventeenth Centuries*, Ann Arbor, 1950.

Wheatley, H. B., ed., *Stow's Survey of London*, London, 1912, (reprinted, 1965).

EASTVVARD
HOE.

As

It was playd in the
Black-friers.

By

The Children of her Maiesties Reuels.

Made by

GEO: CHAPMAN. BEN: IONSON. ION: MARSTON.

 23

AT LONDON
Printed for *William Aspley.*
1605.

see notes on next page

[1–2] *Eastward Hoe*. The cry of Thames boatmen to hail passengers going down-river, i.e. to Greenwich (Court) or Blackwall (harbour). The map, Appendix 1, should help the reader to find places mentioned in the text and notes.

[5] *Black-friers*. A private (enclosed) theatre within the city precinct which catered to a financial if not social élite. Admission charged was 6*d.*, as compared with 1*d.* in the public amphitheatres (e.g. the Globe), and plays were performed 'once a week' (*Epilogue*) rather than daily. As the opening stage direction indicates, there were three stage doors; the middle one was apparently large enough to have been used as a curtained discovery space. The curtain could be pulled shut for scenes taking place 'outside'. The smaller doorways may have been used as parts of the Counter in Act V.

The space 'above', the balcony referred to by Chapman as the *tarras*, in *May-Day*, is used as the upstairs of a house (II, ii, 186) and as the site of the pole at Cuckold's Haven (IV, i)—*Enter* SLITGUT, *with a pair of ox-horns, discovering Cuckold's Haven, above*. It could also have been conveniently used for the appearance of Mistresses Fond and Gazer (III, ii) to prevent overcrowding on the stage, though the text gives no hint of it.

The 'streets' and 'windows' of the *Epilogue* refer to the floor area and galleries of the Blackfriars.

[7] *her Maiesties Revels*. A boys' company granted a patent by James I in 1604, of which Marston was one of the principal shareholders. The company seems to have been increasingly daring in its contemporary, particularly Scots, satire. There was trouble over Daniel's *Philotas* (1604), *Eastward Ho!*, and finally John Day's *Isle of Gulls* (1606), which lost them the queen's patronage because, according to Sir Thomas Hoby's letter (Chambers, op. cit., III, 286), 'from the highest to the lowest, all men's parts were acted by two divers nations'.

[11] *Aspley*. Seems to have taken an interest in Chapman's work, 1604–07. He apparently bought Thorpe's share of this play, for which he was co-signatory in the Stationers' Register.

[DRAMATIS PERSONAE

WILLIAM TOUCHSTONE, *a goldsmith*
MISTRESS TOUCHSTONE, *his wife*
FRANCIS QUICKSILVER ⎱ *his apprentices*
GOLDING ⎰   5
GERTRUDE ⎱ *his daughters*
MILDRED ⎰
BETTRICE, *Mildred's maid*
POLDAVY, *a tailor*
SIR PETRONEL FLASH, *a new-made knight*   10
SECURITY, *an old usurer*
WINIFRED, *his wife*
SINDEFY, *Quicksilver's mistress*
BRAMBLE, *a lawyer*
SEAGULL, *a sea captain*   15
SCAPETHRIFT ⎱ *adventurers bound for Virginia*
SPENDALL ⎰
HAMLET, *a footman*
POTKIN, *a tankard-bearer*
MISTRESS FOND ⎱ *citizens' wives*   20
MISTRESS GAZER ⎰
SLITGUT, *a butcher's apprentice*
WOLF ⎱ *Officers of the Counter*
HOLDFAST ⎰
A SCRIVENER, A COACHMAN, SIR PETRONEL'S PAGE, A DRAWER *at*   25
the Blue Anchor Tavern, MESSENGER, GENTLEMEN, PRISONERS,
FRIEND]

[1] *Dramatis Personae* following H. & S., IV, 523, absent in Q1, 2, and 3.
The names of the principal characters are derived from alchemy.
These names were not only suitable to the prodigal-son story, but also
provided the authors with a shorthand for character traits, and a
formula for interaction. (For a discussion of Jonson's use of names see
G. B. Jackson, *Vision and Judgement in Ben Jonson's Drama* (New
Haven, Conn., 1968), pp. 57–69, and for an interesting summary of
his alchemical ideas see F. H. Mares, Revels edition of Ben Jonson's
The Alchemist (London, 1967), pp. xxxi–xl.)

3

[2] TOUCHSTONE. A smooth, fine-grained variety of black quartz used for testing gold or silver by the colour produced from rubbing upon it. Fig. to try or test the genuineness of anything. Hence his catchphrase, 'work upon that now', i.e., 'test yourself against that'.

[4] QUICKSILVER. Mercury; also sl. for cheat, thief. Its 'nimble-spirited' antics (especially subduing gold) exasperate the alchemist, but the promise of gold or, still better, *lumen novum*, philosophers' gold, helps him to persist. The process of conversion was variously described but consisted basically of: washing, heating (to drive off sulphur), sublimation, and the addition of gold to the fixed metal. Marriage was often symbolic of conversion.

[5] GOLDING. Good as gold and just as malleable in the goldsmith's hands.

[10] SIR PETRONEL FLASH. (Petronel = carbine), i.e., the sound of a gun's report, suggesting the fustian of a blustering gallant.

[11] SECURITY. A humour figure—melancholy: element, earth; metal, sulphur. Unlike Touchstone, encourages Quicksilver's pretensions which he uses as a tracer for gold.

[13] SINDEFY. Befitting one who is Quicksilver's and later Gertrude's foil. Reveals her background: of Puritan stock corrupted to 'Sin' by the city, and 'sweet Sin' (harlot) by Quicksilver.

[17] SPENDALL. Is twice abbreviated *Spoyl*. (III, i, s.p. 52, 61). H. & S., IX, 647 suggest that the name may have been changed to remove unwanted satire.

[18] HAMLET. Brooke and Paradise, op. cit., p. 412, conjecture that he was named for the actor Robert Hamlett, an adult actor by 1611. This might explain 'Gertrude' who is not named for her humour as is her sister 'Mildred'—i.e., mild.

PROLOGUE

Not out of envy, for there's no effect
Where there's no cause; nor out of imitation,
For we have evermore been imitated;
Nor out of our contention to do better
Than that which is opposed to ours in title,   5
For that was good; and better cannot be:
And for the title, if it seem affected,
We might as well have called it, 'God you good even'.
Only that eastward, westwards still exceeds—
Honour the sun's fair rising, not his setting.   10
Nor is our title utterly enforced,
As by the points we touch at, you shall see.
Bear with our willing pains, if dull or witty;
We only dedicate it to the City.

3 *we have evermore been imitated.* Referring to Dekker and Webster's
  imitation of 'city comedy', *Westward Ho!* and *Northward Ho!* A possible
  reference also to the character of Bellamont (Chapman) of *Northward
  Ho!* (See A. Nicholl, 'The Dramatic Portrait of George Chapman',
  PQ, XLI (1962), 215–28.)
5 *opposed to ours in title.* i.e., *Westward Ho!* (Dekker and Webster) performed by the rival Paul's Children in the late autumn or early winter
  of 1604. See E. E. Stoll, *John Webster* (Boston, Mass., 1905), p. 14 and
  M. L. Hunt, *Thomas Dekker. A Study* (Columbia Studies in English,
  1911), pp. 101–2.
8 *God you good even.* Mocking the use of clichés as titles, as in *What You
  Will*, *As You Like It*, etc.
9 *eastward, westwards still exceeds.* Eastward was the traditional direction
  of good luck; 'still exceeds' may be an ironic reference to the residence
  of the Court at Greenwich from mid-March to mid-June 1605. cf.
  Plutarch's *Morals*, 'More men . . . worship the sun rising than . . .
  setting'. See L. Hotson, *Mr. W. H.* (London, 1964), p. 223.
11 *title utterly enforced.* i.e., the values of those whose ambitions are rising
   with the new king are not unconditionally upheld.
14 *We only dedicate it . . . City.* This polite dedication is probably meant
   in the facetious tone of the rest of the *Prologue*.

EASTWARD HO!

Act I, Scene i

[Goldsmith's Row]

Enter MASTER TOUCHSTONE *and* QUICKSILVER *at several doors;*
QUICKSILVER *with his hat, pumps, short sword and dagger, and a
racket trussed up under his cloak. At the middle door, enter*
GOLDING, *discovering a goldsmith's shop, and walking short turns
before it*

TOUCHSTONE

And whither with you now? What loose action are you bound
for? Come, what comrades are you to meet withal? Where's
the supper? Where's the rendezvous?

QUICKSILVER

Indeed, and in very good sober truth, sir—

TOUCHSTONE

'Indeed, and in very good sober truth, sir'! Behind my back   5
thou wilt swear faster than a French foot-boy, and talk more
bawdily than a common midwife; and now, 'indeed, and in
very good sober truth, sir'! But if a privy search should be
made, with what furniture are you rigged now? Sirrah, I
tell thee, I am thy master, William Touchstone, goldsmith;   10
and thou my prentice, Francis Quicksilver; and I will see
whither you are running. 'Work upon that now'!

QUICKSILVER

Why, sir, I hope a man may use his recreation with his
master's profit.

TOUCHSTONE

Prentices' recreations are seldom with their master's profit.   15
'Work upon that now'! You shall give up your cloak, though

1 s.d. *at several doors* different doors. See above, note 5, p. 2
9 *furniture* equipage, embellishment, decoration

---

4 *in very good sober truth.* Mocking Touchstone's euphemisms, as he
does in II, i with 'forsooth'.
6 *French foot-boy.* A page, notorious for his swearing.
16–17 *though you be no alderman.* City statutes dictated the manner and
colour of dress worn by citizens. Aldermen wore red robes; artisans,
flat caps; and apprentices, cap and gown.

you be no alderman. Heyday, Ruffians' Hall! Sword, pumps,
here's a racket indeed!

TOUCHSTONE *uncloaks* QUICKSILVER

QUICKSILVER
'Work upon that now'!

TOUCHSTONE
Thou shameless varlet, dost thou jest at thy lawful master   20
contrary to thy indentures?

QUICKSILVER
Why, 'sblood, sir, my mother's a gentlewoman, and my
father a Justice of Peace, and of Quorum. And though I am
a younger brother and a prentice, yet I hope I am my father's
son; and, by God's lid, 'tis for your worship and for your   25
commodity that I keep company. I am entertained among
gallants, true! They call me cousin Frank, right! I lend them
moneys, good! They spend it, well! But when they are
spent, must not they strive to get more? Must not their land
fly? And to whom? Shall not your worship ha' the refusal?   30
Well, I am a good member of the City, if I were well considered. How would merchants thrive, if gentlemen would
not be unthrifts? How could gentlemen be unthrifts, if their
humours were not fed? How should their humours be fed but
by white-meat and cunning secondings? Well, the City might   35
consider us. I am going to an ordinary now: the gallants fall
to play; I carry light gold with me; the gallants call, 'Cousin
Frank, some gold for silver!'; I change, gain by it; the
gallants lose the gold, and then call, 'Cousin Frank, lend me
some silver!' Why—   40

TOUCHSTONE
Why? I cannot tell. Seven-score pound art thou out in the
cash; but look to it, I will not be gallanted out of my moneys!
And as for my rising by other men's fall; God shield me!

17 *Ruffians' Hall* Ed. (Ruffins hall Q)
34 *humours* dispositions, affectations

17 *Ruffians' Hall*. A field in West Smithfield: site of brawls.
18 *racket*. Tennis racket; and play on the sense racket, a loud noise.
19 s.d. *uncloaks*. Perhaps part of Touchstone's alchemical role; i.e.,
   calcination, removing the glitter.
23 *Justice . . . of Quorum*. A distinguished Justice who presided over a
   'bench'.
36 *ordinary*. Tavern where gallants met to eat, drink, and gamble.
37 *light gold*. Counterfeit money. Its method of preparation is described by
   Quicksilver (IV, i, 202–24).

Did I gain my wealth by ordinaries? No! By exchanging of
gold? No! By keeping of gallants' company? No! I hired me　　45
a little shop, sought low, took small gain, kept no debt-book,
garnished my shop for want of plate, with good wholesome
thrifty sentences, as, 'Touchstone, keep thy shop, and thy
shop will keep thee'. 'Light gains makes heavy purses'. ''Tis
good to be merry and wise'. And when I was wived, having　　50
something to stick to, I had the horn of suretyship ever
before my eyes. You all know the device of the horn, where
the young fellow slips in at the butt-end, and comes squeezed
out at the buckle. And I grew up, and, I praise Providence, I
bear my brows now as high as the best of my neighbours:　　55

46 *sought* ed. (fought Q)
49 *Light gains*, etc. proverbial. Tilley, G7
49–50 *'Tis good*, etc. proverbial. Tilley, G324

51–2 *horn of suretyship . . . device of the horn.* Touchstone alludes to the
notorious method by which London merchants cheated young country
gentlemen of their fortunes and lands. A sixteenth-century panel
(described by J. E. Hodgkin, in *N&Q* (1887), IV, 323-4) illustrates the
moral that 'This horn embleme here doth showe Of suertishipp what
harme doth growe'. The panel shows an enormous horn hanging across
a tree. At the far left stands a wealthy citizen, dressed to suit his
affluence. He supervises a character, dressed like Quicksilver (purple
doublet, profusely slashed; large felt hat and cloak, with a dagger in
his girdle), who is thrusting a victim into the opening of the horn; his
unhappy face and an arm emerging from the narrow end (buckle). The
citizen holds a rope, loosely tied around the victim's legs. To the right
stands another ragged, woebegone, gallant (i.e., the gallant, fleeced). In
William Fennor's seventeenth-century pamphlet, 'The Counter's
Commonwealth', A. V. Judges (ed.), op. cit., pp. 441-8, the emblem is
further elucidated. Citizens would draw in victims by at first refusing
them commodities (the lending of goods by which money could be
raised). This only increased the gallant's determination to get the goods.
The citizen would then send a go-between (probably dressed like
Quicksilver) who would advise the gallant on how to persuade the
merchant to grant him credit. The gallant again approached the merchant who once more stubbornly refused. Finally the merchant agreed,
provided 'an endeared friend' could be found as guarantor. In desperation the gallant would ask the go-between to sign for half the bond.
In order to raise cash quickly the gentleman would then give the goods
to the go-between if the latter would sell them for him. But the gentleman was still totally responsible for the bond, and if he forfeited when
it was due, the citizen would invite him to supper and then have him
arrested. He would only be released on paying back the whole sum,
which usually meant forfeiting his inheritance or ancestral lands.

but thou—well, look to the accounts; your father's bond lies
for you; seven score pound is yet in the rear.

QUICKSILVER

Why, 'slid, sir, I have as good, as proper, gallants' words for
it as any are in London; gentlemen of good phrase, perfect
language, passingly behaved; gallants that wear socks and   60
clean linen, and call me 'kind Cousin Frank', 'good Cousin
Frank'— for they know my father; and, by God's lid, shall
not I trust 'em? Not trust?

Enter a PAGE, *as inquiring for* TOUCHSTONE's *shop*

GOLDING

What do ye lack, sir? What is't you'll buy, sir?

TOUCHSTONE

Ay, marry, sir; there's a youth of another piece. There's thy   65
fellow-prentice, as good a gentleman born as thou art; nay,
and better miened. But does he pump it, or racket it? Well,
if he thrive not, if he outlast not a hundred such crackling
bavins as thou art, God and men neglect industry.

GOLDING

It is his shop, and here my master walks.   70

To the PAGE

TOUCHSTONE

With me, boy?

PAGE

My master, Sir Petronel Flash, recommends his love to you,
and will instantly visit you.

TOUCHSTONE

To make up the match with my eldest daughter, my wife's
dilling, whom she longs to call madam. He shall find me   75
unwillingly ready, boy.   *Exit* PAGE
There's another affliction too. As I have two prentices, the
one of a boundless prodigality, the other of a most hopeful
industry; so have I only two daughters: the eldest, of a

---

67 *miened* ed. (meaned Q)
75 *dilling* darling

---

56 *father's bond*. Obligation to pay a sum of money for an indenture.
62 *by God's lid*. By God's eyelid. Such oaths were banned from the stage
by an act passed in May 1606, offences being subject to a fine of £10.
Eastward Ho! may have been the *cause célèbre*.
64 *What do ye lack*, etc. Tradesman's familiar greeting to his customer.
68-9 *crackling bavins*. Twigs used to ignite a fire. cf. *1 Henry IV*, III, ii,
61-2, 'rash bavin wits, Soon kindled and soon burnt'.

proud ambition and nice wantonness, the other of a modest   80
humility and comely soberness. The one must be ladyfied,
forsooth, and be attired just to the court-cut and long-tail.
So far is she ill-natured to the place and means of my preferment and fortune, that she throws all the contempt and
despite hatred itself can cast upon it. Well, a piece of land   85
she has, 'twas her grandmother's gift: let her, and her Sir
Petronel, flash out that! But as for my substance, she that
scorns me, as I am a citizen and tradesman, shall never
pamper her pride with my industry; shall never use me as
men do foxes: keep themselves warm in the skin, and throw   90
the body that bare it to the dunghill. I must go entertain
this Sir Petronel. Golding, my utmost care's for thee, and
only trust in thee; look to the shop. As for you, Master
Quicksilver, think of husks, for thy course is running
directly to the Prodigals' hogs' trough! Husks, sirrah! 'Work   95
upon that now'!   *Exit* TOUCHSTONE
QUICKSILVER
Marry faugh, goodman flat-cap! 'Sfoot! though I am a
prentice, I can give arms; and my father's a Justice-o'-Peace
by descent; and 'sblood—
GOLDING
Fie, how you swear!   100
QUICKSILVER
'Sfoot man, I am a gentleman, and may swear by my pedi-
gree, God's my life. Sirrah Golding, wilt be ruled by a fool?
Turn good fellow, turn swaggering gallant, and 'Let the
welkin roar, and Erebus also'. Look not westward to the fall
of Don Phoebus, but to the East—Eastward Ho!   105

8 *nice* lascivious, loose
89–90 *as men do foxes*, etc. proverbial. Tilley, M1163
98 *give arms* bear arms, display one's gentlemanly rank
105 *Don Phoebus* the sun

---

82 *court-cut and long-tail.* Alluding to the long flowing gowns worn by
      court ladies; also 'one and all'.
97 *Marry faugh.* Oath of contempt. The name of a bawd in Marston, *The
      Dutch Courtesan* (1605).
97 *flat-cap.* The round cap fashionable in Henry VIII's reign, and later
      characteristic of London merchants and apprentices (see above, note
      I, i, 16–17).
103–4 *Let the welkin roar*, etc. Scraps from Pistol's rant, *2 Henry IV*, II, iv,
      182.

'Where radiant beams of lusty Sol appear,
And bright Eoüs makes the welkin clear'.

We are both gentlemen, and therefore should be no coxcombs; let's be no longer fools to this flat-cap, Touchstone.
Eastward, bully! This satin-belly, and canvas-backed   110
Touchstone—'slife, man, his father was a malt-man, and
his mother sold gingerbread in Christ-church!

GOLDING
What would ye ha' me do?

QUICKSILVER
Why, do nothing, be like a gentleman, be idle; the curse of
man is labour. Wipe thy bum with testons, and make ducks   115
and drakes with shillings. What, Eastward Ho! Wilt thou
cry, 'what is't ye lack?', stand with a bare pate and a dropping
nose under a wooden pent-house, and art a gentleman?
Wilt thou bear tankards, and may'st bear arms? Be ruled,
turn gallant, Eastward Ho! 'Ta ly-re, ly-re ro! Who calls   120
Jeronimo? Speak, here I am!' God's so, how like a sheep
thou look'st! O' my conscience some cowherd begot thee,
thou Golding of Golding Hall, ha, boy?

GOLDING
Go, ye are a prodigal coxcomb; I a cowherd's son, because
I turn not a drunken whore-hunting rake-hell like thyself?   125

---

107 *Eoüs* the dawn.
107 *welkin* sky
115 *testons* sixpences
125 *rake-hell* scoundrel, wanton, debauchee

106–7 *Where . . . clear.* I have been unable to identify this quotation.
110 *bully.* Term implying friendly admiration: fine fellow, gallant.
110 *satin-belly, and canvas-backed.* Tradesmen's dress consisting of satin-
   fronted canvas. Quicksilver may also intend this as an emblem of the
   tradesman's ethic, i.e., soft(-spoken) before, and tough(-minded) after.
115–16 *ducks and drakes.* A game of making flat stones skip across water.
   Proverbial. Tilley, D632.
118 *wooden pent-house.* Awning projecting over the bench outside the
   goldsmith's shop.
119 *bear tankards.* Apprentices' duties included serving their masters with
   water from the conduits or the Thames.
120–1 *Who calls Jeronimo?* Opening line of one of the most famous speeches
   in Kyd's *Spanish Tragedy*, II, v, 4.

QUICKSILVER

Rake-hell! Rake-hell!

Offers to draw, and GOLDING *trips up his heels and holds him*

GOLDING

Pish, in soft terms ye are a cowardly bragging boy, I'll ha'
you whipped.

QUICKSILVER

Whipped? That's good, i'faith. Untruss me?

GOLDING

No, thou wilt undo thyself. Alas, I behold thee with pity,　130
not with anger, thou common shot-clog, gull of all companies! Methinks I see thee already walking in Moorfields
without a cloak, with half a hat, without a band, a doublet
with three buttons, without a girdle, a hose with one point
and no garter, with a cudgel under thine arm, borrowing　135
and begging threepence.

QUICKSILVER

Nay, 'slife, take this and take all! As I am a gentleman born,
I'll be drunk, grow valiant, and beat thee.　　　　*Exit*

GOLDING

Go, thou most madly vain, whom nothing can recover but
that which reclaims atheists, and makes great persons some-　140
times religious: calamity. As for my place and life, thus I
have read:

'Whate'er some vainer youth may term disgrace,
The gain of honest pains is never base;
From trades, from arts, from valour, honour springs;　145
These three are founts of gentry, yea of kings'.

[Retires]

---

127 s.d. *Offers to draw*, etc. This exchange perfectly illustrates the con-
frontation expected in the attack of gold by mercury.

131 *shot-clog*. A dupe who pays the bill (shot) for the whole company at the
tavern.

132 *Moorfields*. The field lying to the north of the city (see Appendix 1 for
location), a famous haunt of beggars. W. Peery shows how Field uses a
similar passage in *A Woman is a Weathercock* (sig. G4ʳ) and suggests
that Field might have played Quicksilver's role in the original production. (*MLN*, LXII (1947), 131–2: 'Zoons! methinks I see myself in
Moorfields, upon a wooden leg, begging threepence'.)

143–6 *Whate'er . . . kings*. No source has been found for these lines of
commonplace seventeenth-century morality.

[Act I, Scene ii

A Room in TOUCHSTONE'*s House*]

Enter GERTRUDE, MILDRED, BETTRICE, *and* POLDAVY, *a tailor;*
POLDAVY *with a fair gown, Scotch farthingale, and French fall in
his arms;* GERTRUDE *in a French head-attire and citizen's gown;*
MILDRED *sewing, and* BETTRICE *leading a monkey after her*

GERTRUDE

For the passion of patience, look if Sir Petronel approach;
that sweet, that fine, that delicate, that—for love's sake, tell
me if he come. O sister Mill, though my father be a low-
capped tradesman, yet I must be a lady; and, I praise God,
my mother must call me Madam. (Does he come?) Off with   5
this gown for shame's sake, off with this gown! Let not my

---

1 s.d. GERTRUDE Ed. (*girted* Q)
   Scotch farthingale Ed. (Scotch Varthingall Q)

---

1 s.d. BETTRICE. Makes her only appearance to utter one line (I, ii, 65).
Parrott suggests she is a visual pun reflecting Gertrude's mimicry of
court manners. Earlier (London, 1822) Nares, *A Glossary*, notes that
ape occasionally meant 'a fool'; it probably meant that those coquettes
who made fools of men would have them still to lead against their will.
Beatrice in *Much Ado About Nothing*, II, i, 37, alludes to 'leading apes
into hell' as the proverbial fate of old maids: hence possibly a visual
emblem for Mildred. This scene may have been cut considerably (see
above, *Note on the Text*, pp. xlii-xliii), so by far the most persuasive argument is H. & S.'s (op. cit., IV, 496), that the passage cut was a s.d. in
which Bettrice makes the monkey perform on the word 'Scot'. cf. Donne,
in his first *Satire*, 79–82: 'He doth move no more/Then . . . thou O
Elephant or Ape wilt doe,/When any names the King of Spaine to you';
or Jonson, in the Induction to *Bartholomew Fair*, who describes an ape
that will 'come over the chaine, for the *King* of *England*, and backe
againe for the *Prince*, and sit still on his arse for the *Pope*, and the *King*
of *Spaine*!' In view of this theory, a s.d. has been inserted by the present
editor at I, ii, 47.
Scotch farthingale. Hooped petticoat popular in Elizabethan and
Jacobean times. Learning to wear a Scotch farthingale is synonymous
with learning to become a miser in *Westward Ho!*, I, i, 35 (Thomas
Dekker, *Dramatic Works*, ed. Fredson Bowers, 4 vols., Cambridge,
1953–61, II.)
French fall. Falling band; i.e., type of collar, softer than the stiff-
standing ruff.
French head-attire. i.e., French hood: headdress worn by women
(*O.E.D.*).

knight take me in the city-cut in any hand. Tear't, pax on't—
does he come?—tear't off! [*Sings*] *Thus whilst she sleeps, I
sorrow for her sake, &c.*

MILDRED

Lord, sister, with what an immodest impatiency and dis- 10
graceful scorn do you put off your city tire; I am sorry to
think you imagine to right yourself in wronging that which
hath made both you and us.

GERTRUDE

I tell you I cannot endure it, I must be a lady: do you wear
your coif with a London licket, your stammel petticoat with 15
two guards, the buffin gown with the tuf-taffety cape, and
the velvet lace. I must be a lady, and I will be a lady. I like
some humours of the city dames well: to eat cherries only
at an angel a pound, good. To dye rich scarlet black, pretty.
To line a grogram gown clean through with velvet, tolerable. 20
Their pure linen, their smocks of three pound a smock, are
to be borne withal. But your mincing niceries, taffeta
pipkins, durance petticoats, and silver bodkins—God's my
life, as I shall be a lady, 1 cannot endure it! Is he come yet?

---

7 *in any hand* in any case
21 *smock* woman's undergarment
23 *pipkins* hats
23 *durance* a stout durable cloth (*O.E.D.*)

---

7 *pax.* Euphemism for pox, i.e., syphilis.
8–9 *Thus whilst she sleeps*, etc. From the song beginning 'Sleep wayward
thoughts' (Dowland, *First Book of Songs* (1597), ed. Fellowes in *The
English School of Lutenist Song Writers*, London, 1921, II, 50–2).
15 *licket.* Lace or ribbon used to tie on coifs.
15 *stammel.* Cheap red woollen cloth worn by the lower classes.
16 *guards.* Ornamental trimming, not lavish enough for Gertrude's
extravagant tastes.
16 *buffin.* Coarse woollen grosgrain; cf. Massinger, *The City Madam*,
IV, iv, 26, where the ruined upstarts appear 'in buffin gowns'.
16 *tuf-taffety.* 'Plain taffeta was not rich enough for Elizabethan taste. It
must be "tufted", i.e. woven with raised stripes or spots' (M. C.
Linthicum, *Costume in the Drama of Shakespeare and His Contempor-
aries*, Oxford, 1936, p. 124); quoted H. & S., IX, 651.
18 *to eat cherries*, etc. The extravagance of city dames in paying 10
shillings a pound for cherries is satirized also in Dekker's *Batchelor's
Banquet* (1603) (Thomas Dekker, *Non Dramatic Works*, ed. A. B.
Grossart, 5 vols., London, 1884–86, I, 173).
23 *bodkin.* A long pin or pin-shaped ornament used by women to fasten up
the hair.

Lord, what a long knight 'tis! [*Sings*] *And ever she cried,*   25
Shoot home!—and yet I knew one longer—*And ever she cried,*
Shoot home! Fa, la, ly, re, lo, la!

MILDRED
Well, sister, those that scorn their nest, oft fly with a sick
wing.

GERTRUDE
Bow-bell!   30

MILDRED
Where titles presume to thrust before fit means to second
them, wealth and respect often grow sullen and will not
follow. For sure in this, I would for your sake I spoke not
truth: 'Where ambition of place goes before fitness of birth,
contempt and disgrace follow'. I heard a scholar once say   35
that Ulysses, when he counterfeited himself mad, yoked
cats and foxes and dogs together to draw his plough, whilst
he followed and sowed salt; but sure I judge them truly
mad that yoke citizens and courtiers, tradesmen and soldiers,
a goldsmith's daughter and a knight. Well, sister, pray God   40
my father sow not salt too.

GERTRUDE
Alas! Poor Mill, when I am a lady, I'll pray for thee yet,
i'faith: nay, and I'll vouchsafe to call thee Sister Mill still;
for though thou art not like to be a lady as I am, yet sure
thou art a creature of God's making, and mayest peradven-   45
ture to be saved as soon as I—does he come?
                    [*Sings, and monkey cartwheels*]
And ever and anon she doubled in her song.
Now, Lady's my comfort, what a profane ape's here!

26, 27 *Shoot* Ed. (*shout* Q)
28–9 *those that . . . wing* proverbial. Tilley, B377

25–7 *And ever she cried*, etc. An unidentified ballad with markedly sexual
    overtones.
30 *Bow-bell.* Term for a cockney, i.e., one born within the sound of the
    bells of St Mary-le-Bow Church in Cheapside (often pejorative).
    Proverbial. Tilley, S671.
36–8 *Ulysses . . . salt.* Mildred here misinterprets the scholar; to feign
    madness, Ulysses yoked together an ass and an ox, then ploughed sand
    and sowed salt.
47 s.d. H. & S., IV, 496 suggest that here (A4ᵛ) 'nine lines have been
    excised from the text . . .' though 'a vestige of a gibe against the Scotch
    survives'. (See above, note, I, ii, 1 s.d., and *Note on the Text*, pp. xlii–xliii.)
47 *doubled.* Repeated a note higher (Brooke and Paradise, op. cit. p. 402.).
48 *Lady's my comfort*, etc. Ref. to Virgin Mary as By'r' Lady.

Tailor, Poldavis, prithee, fit it, fit it! Is this a right Scot?
Does it clip close, and bear up round?   50

POLDAVY
Fine and stiffly, i'faith; 'twill keep your thighs so cool, and
make your waist so small; here was a fault in your body, but
I have supplied the defect with the effect of my steel instru-
ment, which, though it have but one eye, can see to rectify
the imperfection of the proportion.   55

GERTRUDE
Most edifying tailor! I protest you tailors are most sanc-
tified members, and make many crooked things go upright.
How must I bear my hands? Light, light?

POLDAVY
O, ay, now you are in the lady-fashion, you must do all
things light. Tread light, light. Ay, and fall so: that's the   60
court-amble.

She trips about the stage

GERTRUDE
Has the Court ne'er a trot?

POLDAVY
No, but a false gallop, lady.

GERTRUDE
And if she will not go to bed,—

Cantat

BETTRICE
The knight's come, forsooth.   65

Enter SIR PETRONEL, MASTER TOUCHSTONE, *and* MISTRESS
TOUCHSTONE

GERTRUDE
Is my knight come? O the Lord, my band? Sister, do my
cheeks look well? Give me a little box o' the ear that I may
seem to blush; now, now. So, there, there, there! Here he
is! O my dearest delight! Lord, Lord, and how does my
knight?   70

49–50 *Scot . . . round* refers to the Scotch farthingale
57 *things* Ed. (thing Q)
61 *amble* artificial or acquired pace (*N.E.D.*)
65 s.d. *Cantat* she sings
66 *band* husband, and possible pun on falling band

51–5 *Fine . . . proportion.* This *double entendre* in the mouth of the tailor is
    predictable, since tailors were reputedly lecherous.
64 *And . . . bed.* I have been unable to identify this song.

3

TOUCHSTONE

Fie, with more modesty!

GERTRUDE

Modesty! Why, I am no citizen now—modesty! Am I not
to be married? Y'are best to keep me modest, now I am to
be a lady.

SIR PETRONEL

Boldness is good fashion and courtlike.   75

GERTRUDE

Ay, in a country lady I hope it is; as I shall be. And how
chance ye came no sooner, Knight?

SIR PETRONEL

'Faith, I was so entertained in the progress with one Count
Epernoum, a Welsh knight; we had a match at balloon too
with my Lord Whachum, for four crowns.   80

GERTRUDE

At baboon? Jesu! You and I will play at baboon in the
country, Knight?

SIR PETRONEL

O, sweet lady, 'tis a strong play with the arm.

GERTRUDE

With arm or leg or any other member, if it be a court sport.
And when shall's be married, my Knight?   85

SIR PETRONEL

I come now to consummate it, and your father may call a
poor knight son-in-law.

TOUCHSTONE

Sir, ye are come. What is not mine to keep, I must not be
sorry to forgo. A hundred pound land her grandmother left
her, 'tis yours; herself (as her mother's gift) is yours. But if   90
you expect aught from me, know, my hand and mine eyes
open together: I do not give blindly. 'Work upon that now'!

SIR PETRONEL

Sir, you mistrust not my means! I am a knight.

79 *Epernoum*. This may be a personal gibe; a Count Peppernoun appears in
   Northward Ho!
79 *balloon*. A game like football, but played entirely in the air with 'bracers',
   flat pieces of wood attached to the arm.
89 *A hundred pound land*. Refers to the yearly income accruing from the
   property. Touchstone's valuation of 'two thousand pounds' worth of
   good land' (IV, ii, 232–3) gives the market value of the estate, including
   'two hundred pounds' worth of wood ready to fell; and a fine sweet
   house . . .' (II, ii, 135–8).

TOUCHSTONE

Sir, sir, what I know not, you will give me leave to say I am
ignorant of.   95

MISTRESS TOUCHSTONE

Yes, that he is a knight; I know where he had money to pay
the gentlemen-ushers and heralds their fees. Ay, that he is
a knight; and so might you have been, too, if you had been
aught else than an ass, as well as some of your neighbours.
And I thought you would not ha' been knighted (as I am an   100
honest woman), I would ha' dubbed you myself. I praise
God I have wherewithal. But as for you, daughter—

GERTRUDE

Ay, mother, I must be a lady tomorrow; and by your leave,
mother (I speak it not without my duty, but only in the right
of my husband), I must take place of you, mother.   105

MISTRESS TOUCHSTONE

That you shall, Lady-daughter, and have a coach as well as
I too.

GERTRUDE

Yes, mother. But by your leave, mother (I speak it not
without my duty, but only in my husband's right), my
coach-horses must take the wall of your coach-horses.   110

TOUCHSTONE

Come, come, the day grows low: 'tis supper-time. Use my
house; the wedding solemnity is at my wife's cost; thank
me for nothing but my willing blessing, for (I cannot feign)
my hopes are faint. And, sir, respect my daughter; she has
refused for you wealthy and honest matches, known good   115
men, well-moneyed, better traded, best reputed.

GERTRUDE

Body o' truth, 'chitizens, chitizens'. Sweet Knight, as soon
as ever we are married, take me to thy mercy out of this
miserable 'chity', presently, carry me out of the scent of

118 *to* Ed. (to to Q)

96–7 *I know where he had money*, etc. Refers to the sale of knighthoods. A
    grant of 29 May 1604 fixed the fees paid to the gentlemen-ushers,
    heralds-at-arms, etc.

110 *take the wall*. Have precedence, i.e., the person who walked on the
    outside of the pavement would have to endure the garbage thrown from
    the upstairs windows of the house.

117 *chitizens*. Affected pronunciation of city-dames. (*Eastward Ho!*, ed.
    A. H. Bullen, *The Works of John Marston*, 3 vols., London, 1887,
    III, 1–124.) This speech seems to parody the language of *Westward Ho!*

Newcastle coal, and the hearing of Bow-bell, I beseech thee,   120
down with me, for God's sake!

TOUCHSTONE
Well, daughter, I have read, that old wit sings:
  'The greatest rivers flow from little springs.
  Though thou art full, scorn not thy means at first;
  He that's most drunk may soonest be athirst'.   125
'Work upon that now'!

All but TOUCHSTONE, MILDRED *and* GOLDING *depart*
No, no! Yond' stand my hopes. Mildred, come hither
daughter. And how approve you your sister's fashion? How
do you fancy her choice? What dost thou think?

MILDRED
I hope, as a sister, well.   130

TOUCHSTONE
Nay but, nay but, how dost thou like her behaviour and
humour? Speak freely.

MILDRED
I am loath to speak ill; and yet, I am sorry of this, I cannot
speak well.

TOUCHSTONE
Well! Very good, as I would wish; a modest answer.   135
Golding, come hither; hither, Golding! How dost thou like
the knight, Sir Flash? Does he not look big? How lik'st thou
the elephant? He says he has a castle in the country.

GOLDING
Pray heaven, the elephant carry not his castle on his back.

TOUCHSTONE
'Fore heaven, very well! But, seriously, how dost repute   140
him?

GOLDING
The best I can say of him is, I know him not.

TOUCHSTONE
Ha, Golding! I commend thee, I approve thee, and will
make it appear my affection is strong to thee. My wife has
her humour, and I will ha' mine. Dost thou see my daughter   145

123 *The greatest rivers*, etc. proverbial. Tilley, B681

---

139 *Pray heaven . . . back.* Golding fears that Petronel's only possessions
are his clothes. The elephant in the Middle Ages was frequently repre-
sented with a castle on his back. cf. the chess piece, and the district in
South London. To the Elizabethans the elephant and castle was a
well-known pageant. See Robert Whithington, 'A Note on *Eastward
Ho,* I, ii, 178,' *MLN,* XLIII (1928), 28–9.

here? She is not fair, well-favoured or so, indifferent, which
modest measure of beauty shall not make it thy only work
to watch her, nor sufficient mischance, to suspect her. Thou
art towardly, she is modest; thou art provident, she is careful.
She's now mine: give me thy hand, she's now thine. 'Work   150
upon that now'!

GOLDING
Sir, as your son, I honour you; and as your servant, obey
you.

TOUCHSTONE
Sayest thou so? Come hither, Mildred. Do you see yond'
fellow? He is a gentleman, though my prentice, and has   155
somewhat to take to; a youth of good hope, well-friended,
well parted. Are you mine? You are his. 'Work you upon
that now'!

MILDRED
Sir, I am all yours; your body gave me life; your care and
love, happiness of life; let your virtue still direct it, for to 160
your wisdom I wholly dispose myself.

TOUCHSTONE
Sayest thou so? Be you two better acquainted. Lip her, lip
her, knave! So, shut up shop, in! We must make holiday!
                          Exeunt GOLDING *and* MILDRED
  'This match shall on, for I intend to prove
  Which thrives the best, the mean or lofty love.   165
  Whether fit wedlock vowed 'twixt like and like,
  Or prouder hopes, which daringly o'erstrike
  Their place and means. 'Tis honest time's expense,
  When seeming lightness bears a moral sense'.
  'Work upon that now'!   170
                                                    Exit

---

157 *well parted*. i.e., furnished with good parts or abilities, talented.
168 *'Tis honest time's expense*. Time is used profitably.

Act II, Scene i

[Goldsmith's Row]

TOUCHSTONE, GOLDING, *and* MILDRED, *sitting on either side of the stall*

TOUCHSTONE

Quicksilver! Master Francis Quicksilver! Master Quicksilver!

Enter QUICKSILVER

QUICKSILVER

Here, sir—ump!

TOUCHSTONE

So, sir; nothing but flat Master Quicksilver (without any familiar addition) will fetch you! Will you truss my points,   5
sir?

QUICKSILVER

Ay, forsooth—ump!

TOUCHSTONE

How now, sir? The drunken hiccup so soon this morning?

QUICKSILVER

'Tis but the coldness of my stomach, forsooth.

TOUCHSTONE

What, have you the cause natural for it? Y'are a very learned   10
drunkard; I believe I shall miss some of my silver spoons with
your learning. The nuptial night will not moisten your
throat sufficiently, but the morning likewise must rain her
dews into your gluttonous weasand.

QUICKSILVER

An't please you, sir, we did but drink—ump!—to the   15
coming off of the knightly bridegroom.

TOUCHSTONE

To the coming off on him?

QUICKSILVER

Ay, forsooth! We drunk to his coming on—ump!—when
we went to bed; and now we are up, we must drink to his

1 s.d. omit QUICKSILVER ed.
14 *weasand* gullet

4–5 *without any familiar addition.* cf. Quicksilver's insolent words of
address, 'now I tell thee, Touchstone' (II, i, 120).

5 *truss my points.* The points or laces fastened the doublet to the hose. It
was one of a valet's duties to 'truss' or tie the points.

18–20 *coming on . . . coming off.* Successful completion of the marriage
ritual.

coming off; for that's the chief honour of a soldier, sir; and   20
therefore we must drink so much the more to it, forsooth—
ump!

TOUCHSTONE

A very capital reason! So that you go to bed late, and rise
early to commit drunkenness; you fulfil the Scripture very
sufficient wickedly, forsooth!   25

QUICKSILVER

The knight's men, forsooth, be still o' their knees at it—
ump!—and because 'tis for your credit, sir, I would be loath
to flinch.

TOUCHSTONE

I pray, sir, e'en to 'em again, then; y'are one of the separated
crew, one of my wife's faction, and my young lady's, with   30
whom, and with their great match, I will have nothing to do.

QUICKSILVER

So, sir; now I will go keep my—ump!—credit with 'em, an't
please you, sir!

TOUCHSTONE

In any case, sir, lay one cup of sack more o' your cold
stomach, I beseech you!   35

QUICKSILVER

Yes, forsooth!

                                                    Exit QUICKSILVER

TOUCHSTONE

This is for my credit; servants ever maintain drunkenness
in their master's house, for their master's credit; a good idle
serving-man's reason. I thank Time the night is past! I
ne'er waked to such cost; I think we have stowed more sorts   40
of flesh in our bellies than ever Noah's Ark received; and
for wine, why, my house turns giddy with it, and more noise
in it than at a conduit. Ay me, even beasts condemn our
gluttony! Well, 'tis our City's fault, which, because we
commit seldom, we commit the more sinfully; we lose no   45

---

24 *the Scripture.* Isaiah V, 11—'Woe unto them that rise up early in the
   morning, that they may follow strong drink; that tarry into the night,
   till wine inflame them'.

29–30 *separated crew.* i.e., faction separated from the chosen people.

41 *Noah's Ark.* 'Curious gluttony ransackes, as it were, *Noahs Ark* for food,
   onely to feed the riot of one meale'. (W. J. D. Paylor, ed., *The Over-
   burian Characters*, Oxford, 1936, p. 78.)

43 *conduit.* Here Touchstone alludes to city feasts when the conduits
   (cisterns) were filled with wine.

time in our sensuality, but we make amends for it. O that
we would do so in virtue and religious negligences! But see,
here are all the sober parcels my house can show. I'll eaves-
drop, hear what thoughts they utter this morning.

[He retires]

GOLDING [*and* MILDRED *come forward*]

GOLDING

But is it possible, that you, seeing your sister preferred to   50
the bed of a knight, should contain your affections in the
arms of a prentice?

MILDRED

I had rather make up the garment of my affections in some
of the same piece, than, like a fool, wear gowns of two colours,
or mix sackcloth with satin.   55

GOLDING

And do the costly garments; the title and fame of a lady,
the fashion, observation, and reverence proper to such preferment, no more enflame you, than such convenience as my
poor means and industry can offer to your virtues?

MILDRED

I have observed that the bridle given to those violent flat-   60
teries of fortune is seldom recovered; they bear one headlong
in desire from one novelty to another, and where those
ranging appetites reign, there is ever more passion than
reason; no stay, and so no happiness. These hasty advance-
ments are not natural; Nature hath given us legs to go to our   65
objects, not wings to fly to them.

GOLDING

How dear an object you are to my desires I cannot express;
whose fruition would my master's absolute consent and
yours vouchsafe me, I should be absolutely happy. And
though it were a grace so far beyond my merit, that I should   70
blush with unworthiness to receive it, yet thus far both my
love and my means shall assure your requital: you shall
want nothing fit for your birth and education; what increase
of wealth and advancement the honest and orderly industry
and skill of our trade will afford in any, I doubt not will be   75

50 s.d. GOLDING [*and* MILDRED *come forward*] ed. (*Enter* Golding Q)
60 *bridle* fig. restraint, propriety

46–7 *O that we would do so in virtue and religious negligences.* i.e., Touchstone
    wishes that it were as natural for citizens to make up for their 'virtuous
    and religious negligences' by indulgence in prayer as it was for them to
    compensate for hard work by losing themselves in drink.

aspired by me. I will ever make your contentment the end of
my endeavours; I will love you above all; and only your
grief shall be my misery, and your delight my felicity.

TOUCHSTONE

'Work upon that now'! By my hopes, he woos honestly and
orderly; he shall be anchor of my hopes! Look, see the ill-   80
yoked monster, his fellow!

Enter QUICKSILVER *unlaced, a towel about his neck, in
his flat cap, drunk*

QUICKSILVER

Eastward Ho! 'Holla ye pampered jades of Asia!'

TOUCHSTONE

Drunk now downright, o' my fidelity!

QUICKSILVER

Ump!—Pulldo, pulldo! Showse, quoth the caliver.

GOLDING

Fie, fellow Quicksilver, what a pickle are you in!   85

QUICKSILVER

Pickle? Pickle in thy throat; zounds, pickle! Wa, ha, ho!
Good-morrow, Knight Petronel; 'morrow, lady goldsmith;
come off, Knight, with a counter-buff, for the honour of
knighthood.

GOLDING

Why, how now, sir? Do ye know where you are?   90

QUICKSILVER

Where I am? Why, 'sblood, you jolthead, where I am?

GOLDING

Go to, go to, for shame, go to bed and sleep out this im-
modesty: thou sham'st both my master and his house!

QUICKSILVER

Shame? What shame? I thought thou wouldst show thy
bringing-up; and thou wert a gentleman as I am, thou   95
wouldst think it no shame to be drunk. Lend me some

80–1 *ill-yoked* ill-matched, or ill-mated
84 *Pulldo . . . caliver* bang went the musket (Schelling)
85 *pickle* a sorry plight; a predicament. Proverbial. Tilley, P 276
88 *counter-buff* returned blow
91 *jolthead* blockhead

---

82 s.d. *unlaced.* Points untied, probably doublet undone.
82 *Holla ye pampered jades of Asia!* 2 *Tamburlaine,* IV, iii, 1; parodying
   Marlowe's tragic rant. Also in Pistol's speech, 2 *Henry IV* (II, iv, 178).
86 *Wa, ha, ho!* Cry of a falconer to the falcon; Cocledemoy's catch-phrase
   in *The Dutch Courtesan.*

money, save my credit; I must dine with the serving-men
and their wives—and their wives, sirrah!

GOLDING
E'en who you will; I'll not lend thee threepence.

QUICKSILVER
'Sfoot, lend me some money! 'Hast thou not Hiren here?'   100

TOUCHSTONE
Why, how now, sirrah, what vein's this, ha?

QUICKSILVER
'Who cries on murther? Lady, was it you?' How does our
master? Pray thee, cry Eastward Ho!

TOUCHSTONE
Sirrah, sirrah, y'are past your hiccup now; I see y'are
drunk—   105

QUICKSILVER
'Tis for your credit, master.

TOUCHSTONE
And hear you keep a whore in town—

QUICKSILVER
'Tis for your credit, master.

TOUCHSTONE
And what you are out in cash, I know.

QUICKSILVER
So do I. My father's a gentleman; 'work upon that now'!   110
Eastward Ho!

TOUCHSTONE
Sir, Eastward Ho will make you go Westward Ho. I will no
longer dishonest my house, nor endanger my stock with
your licence. There, sir, there's your indenture; all your
apparel (that I must know) is on your back; and from this   115
time my door is shut to you: from me be free; but for other
freedom, and the moneys you have wasted, Eastward Ho
shall not serve you.

100 *Hiren* siren, seductive woman
113 *dishonest* dishonour
116–17 *other freedom* i.e., making free

---

100 *Hast thou not Hiren here?* A line from a play also quoted by Pistol in
    2 Henry IV (II, iv, 173). Bullen believes it originated in Greene's lost
    play *Mahomet and the Fair Greek Hiren*.
102 *Who cries on murther?* Chapman, *Blind Beggar of Alexandria*, IX, 49.
112 *Westward Ho*. i.e., to the gallows at Tyburn.
114 *indenture*. The contract by which an apprentice is bound to a master
    for seven years to learn the trade.

QUICKSILVER
  Am I free o' my fetters? Rent, fly with a duck in thy mouth!
  And now I tell thee, Touchstone—   120
TOUCHSTONE
  Good sir—
QUICKSILVER
  'When this eternal substance of my soul'—
TOUCHSTONE
  Well said; change your gold-ends for your play-ends.
QUICKSILVER
  'Did live imprisoned in my wanton flesh'—
TOUCHSTONE
  What then, sir?   125
QUICKSILVER
  'I was a courtier in the Spanish Court,
  And Don Andrea was my name'—
TOUCHSTONE
  Good master Don Andrea, will you march?
QUICKSILVER
  Sweet Touchstone, will you lend me two shillings?
TOUCHSTONE
  Not a penny!   130
QUICKSILVER
  Not a penny? I have friends, and I have acquaintance; I will
  piss at thy shop posts, and throw rotten eggs at thy sign.
  'Work upon that now'!
                                                    Exit staggering
TOUCHSTONE
  Now, sirrah, you, hear you? You shall serve me no more
  neither; not an hour longer!   135

126–7 Prose Q

---

119 *Rent, fly with a duck in thy mouth!* Quicksilver inverts the usual meaning
     of this commercial phrase, i.e., return with a good profit, to mean, as
     H. & S. gloss, 'a good riddance, with a profit to myself'.
122, 124, 126–7 *When . . . soul, Did . . . flesh, I . . . name.* From the opening
     speech of Kyd's *Spanish Tragedy*, I, i, INDUCTION.
                              Enter the Ghost of Andrea, and with him Revenge
     GHOST
        When this eternal substance of my soul
        Did live imprison'd in my wanton flesh,
        Each in their function serving other's need,
        I was a courtier in the Spanish court.
        My name was Don Andrea, . . .
123 *gold-ends.* Basic unit of the goldsmith's trade; also moral tags.

GOLDING

What mean you, sir?

TOUCHSTONE

I mean to give thee thy freedom, and with thy freedom my
daughter, and with my daughter a father's love. And with all
these such a portion as shall make Knight Petronel himself
envy thee! Y'are both agreed, are ye not?   140

BOTH

With all submission, both of thanks and duty.

TOUCHSTONE

Well, then, the great power of heaven bless and confirm you.
And Golding, that my love to thee may not show less than
my wife's love to my eldest daughter, thy marriage-feast
shall equal the knight's and hers.   145

GOLDING

Let me beseech you, no, sir; the superfluity and cold meat
left at their nuptials will with bounty furnish ours. The
grossest prodigality is superfluous cost of the belly; nor would
I wish any invitement of states or friends, only your reverent
presence and witness shall sufficiently grace and confirm us. 150

TOUCHSTONE

Son to mine own bosom, take her and my blessing. The nice
fondling, my lady, sir-reverence, that I must not now
presume to call daughter, is so ravished with desire to hansel
her new coach, and see her knight's eastward castle, that
the next morning will sweat with her busy setting-forth.   155
Away will she and her mother, and while their preparation
is making, ourselves, with some two or three other friends,
will consummate the humble match we have in God's name
concluded.

   ''Tis to my wish, for I have often read,   160
Fit birth, fit age, keeps long a quiet bed.
'Tis to my wish: for tradesmen (well 'tis known)
Get with more ease than gentry keeps his own'.

                                 Exeunt

141 s.p. BOTH ed. (*Ambo.* Q)   146 s.p. *Goul* Qq (*Con.* Q)
149 *states* men of rank or dignity (*O.E.D.*)
152 *fondling* a fond or foolish person (*O.E.D.*)
153 *hansel* inaugurate   164 s.d. *Exeunt* Ed. (*Exit* Q)

146 *cold meat*, etc. Parody of *Hamlet* (I, ii, 179–81):
    'Thrift, thrift, Horatio. The funeral baked meats
    Did coldly furnish forth the marriage tables'.
152 *sir-reverence*. 'Save your reverence', with doubtful allusion to sense of
    'excrement'. Brooke and Paradise, op. cit., gloss 'with apologies'.

[Act II, Scene ii

A Room in SECURITY'*s House*]

SECURITY *solus*

SECURITY

My privy guest, lusty Quicksilver, has drunk too deep of
the bride-bowl; but with a little sleep, he is much recovered;
and, I think, is making himself ready to be drunk in a gallanter likeness. My house is, as 'twere, the cave where the
young outlaw hoards the stolen vails of his occupation; and   5
here, when he will revel it in his prodigal similitude, he
retires to his trunks, and (I may say softly) his punks: he
dares trust me with the keeping of both; for I am Security
itself; my name is Security, the famous usurer.

Enter QUICKSILVER *in his prentice's coat and cap, his gallant breeches and stockings, gartering himself;* SECURITY
following

QUICKSILVER

Come, old Security, thou father of destruction! Th' indented   10
sheepskin is burned wherein I was wrapped; and I am now
loose, to get more children of perdition into thy usurous
bonds. Thou feed'st my lechery, and I thy covetousness;
thou art pander to me for my wench, and I to thee for thy
cozenages: 'Ka me, ka thee', runs through court and country.   15

SECURITY

Well said, my subtle Quicksilver! These K's ope the doors

3–4 *gallanter likeness* more finely dressed, more showy in appearance
5 *vails* tips, over and above wages
7 *punks* prostitutes
10–11 *indented sheepskin* indenture
15 *cozenages* cheating, deception, fraud
15 *Ka me, ka thee* Ed. (K. me, K. thee Q)
15 *Ka me, ka thee* proverbial. Tilley, K1. One good turn deserves
   another
16 *K's* pronounced 'keys'

---

7 *trunks.* Short breeches of silk or other material (*O.E.D.*). By city
   regulations, it was illegal for an apprentice to store his apparel outside
   his master's house.
10 s.d. The contrived nature of the above utterance and Security's direction here, when he is already on stage, make it appear probable that
   Security's little set speech was inserted after staging had shown the
   passage following insufficient.

to all this world's felicity; the dullest forehead sees it. Let
not master courtier think he carries all the knavery on his
shoulders: I have known poor Hob in the country, that has
worn hob-nails on's shoes, have as much villainy in's head   20
as he that wears gold buttons in's cap.

QUICKSILVER
Why, man, 'tis the London high-way to thrift; if virtue be
used, 'tis but as a scrap to the net of villainy. They that use it
simply, thrive simply, I warrant. 'Weight and fashion makes
goldsmiths cuckolds'.   25

Enter SINDEFY, *with* QUICKSILVER'*s doublet, cloak, rapier,
and dagger*

SINDEFY
Here, sir, put off the other half of your prenticeship.
QUICKSILVER
Well said, sweet Sin! Bring forth my bravery.
Now let my trunks shoot forth their silks concealed,
I now am free, and now will justify
My trunks and punks. Avaunt, dull flat-cap, then!   30
Via the curtain that shadowed Borgia!
There lie, thou husk of my envassaled state,
I, Samson, now have burst the Philistines' bands,
And in thy lap, my lovely Dalida,
I'll lie, and snore out my enfranchised state.   35
                                        [*Sings*]

19 *Hob* stock term for farm labourer
31 *Via* away

---

23 '*tis but as a scrap in the net of villainy.* Meaning virtue can be a bait with
which the gallant is drawn into the usurer's trap; i.e., Quicksilver pretends
friendship towards gallants, lends them money, and then, by pretending
debt of his own, gets them to sign a bond to Security for a commodity
or an exorbitantly high-interest loan for which they, not he, will be
responsible. See I, i, 51–2 *Suretyship* and A. V. Judges op. cit.,
pp. 448–51.
28 *trunks shoot forth.* Play on the meaning trunks: peashooters.
28 *their silks concealed.* The outer fabric slashed or cut in ribbons to reveal
bright silks beneath.
31 *Via the curtain that shadowed Borgia.* Most eds. ascribe this passage to
Mason's *The Turk*, but as Parrott astutely notes, *The Turk* was not on
the stage until 1607–08. It probably alludes to Cesare Borgia, who at
an early age cast aside the 'curtain' of his clerical state for soldierly
ambition.
34 *Dalida.* From the Greek Bible; Dalila.

'When Samson was a tall young man,
His power and strength increased then';
He sold no more nor cup nor can,
But did them all despise.
Old Touchstone, now write to thy friends   40
For one to sell thy base gold-ends;
Quicksilver now no more attends
Thee, Touchstone.
But, Dad, hast thou seen my running gelding dressed today?
SECURITY
That I have, Frank. The ostler o' th' Cock dressed him for   45
a breakfast.
QUICKSILVER
What, did he eat him?
SECURITY
No, but he eat his breakfast for dressing him; and so dressed
him for breakfast.
QUICKSILVER
'O witty age, where age is young in wit,   50
And all youth's words have gray beards full of it'!
SINDEFY
But alas, Frank, how will all this be maintained now? Your
place maintained it before.
QUICKSILVER
Why, and I maintained my place. I'll to the Court, another
manner of place for maintenance, I hope, than the silly City! 55
I heard my father say, I heard my mother sing an old song
and a true: 'Thou art a she fool, and know'st not what
belongs to our male wisdom'. I shall be a merchant, forsooth,
trust my estate in a wooden trough as he does! What are these
ships but tennis-balls for the winds to play withal? Tossed   60
from one wave to another: now under-line, now over the
house; sometimes brick-walled against a rock, so that the

37 *then* Ed. (*than* Q)
45 *Cock* a tavern
50 *young in wit* vigorous
57 *Thou* Ed. (*Tou* Q)
62 *brick-walled* caused to rebound back (*O.E.D.*)

36–7 *When Samson*, etc. An old Roxburghe Ballad (Stationers' Register,
1563). See W. Chappell, *Popular Music of Olden Time*, 2 vols. (London,
1885–89) I, 241.
61 *under-line*. Tennis allusion: too low for play.
61–2 *over the house*. Sloping roof of the penthouse at one side and two ends
of the court, hence too high for play.

guts fly out again; sometimes struck under the wide hazard, and farewell, master merchant!

SINDEFY

Well, Frank, well; the seas, you say, are uncertain; but he   65
that sails in your court seas shall find 'em ten times fuller of
hazard; wherein to see what is to be seen is torment more
than a free spirit can endure. But when you come to suffer,
how many injuries swallow you! What care and devotion
must you use to humour an imperious lord: proportion your   70
looks to his looks, [your] smiles to his smiles, fit your sails
to the wind of his breath!

QUICKSILVER

Tush, he's no journeyman in his craft that cannot do that!

SINDEFY

But he's worse than a prentice that does it; not only humour-
ing the lord, but every trencher-bearer, every groom that   75
by indulgence and intelligence crept into his favour, and by
panderism into his chamber: he rules the roost; and when
my honourable lord says, 'it shall be thus', my worshipful
rascal, the groom of his close stool, says, 'it shall not be thus',
claps the door after him, and who dares enter? A prentice,   80
quoth you? 'Tis but to learn to live; and does that disgrace
a man? He that rises hardly, stands firmly; but he that rises
with ease, alas, falls as easily!

QUICKSILVER

A pox on you! Who taught you this morality?

SECURITY

'Tis long of this witty age, Master Francis. But indeed,   85
Mistress Sindefy, all trades complain of inconvenience, and

---

63 *hazard* risk
71 *your* Ed. (not in Q)
85 *long of* owing to, on account of

---

63 *under the wide hazard.* Pun—strike the ball wide, and take a risk.
75 *groom.* From the appearance of C1ᵛ in Q, it is possible that something has
been struck from this passage by the printer—probably another jest about
the Scots. It is interesting to note that Sir John Murray, groom of the
king's bedchamber, was the brother of the Sir James Murray who,
according to Jonson, reported the offence to the king. It is also suspicious
that in late 1605 the said John Murray received a large sum of money
from Salisbury, one of the nobles to whom both Jonson and Chapman
appealed from prison in 1605.
80–3 *A prentice,* etc. These words fit awkwardly into Sindefy's speech.
Apart from the innuendo they appear to mean, 'slowly but surely wins'.
It is possible that this is another of the printer's stop-gaps.

therefore 'tis best to have none. The merchant, he complains
and says, 'traffic is subject to much uncertainty and loss'.
Let 'em keep their goods on dry land, with a vengeance, and
not expose other men's substances to the mercy of the winds,   90
under protection of a wooden wall (as Master Francis says);
and all for greedy desire to enrich themselves with uncon-
scionable gain, two for one, or so; where I, and such other
honest men as live by lending money, are content with
moderate profit—thirty or forty i' th' hundred—so we may   95
have it with quietness, and out of peril of wind and weather,
rather than run those dangerous courses of trading as they
do.

                                        [SINDEFY *retires*]
QUICKSILVER
Ay, Dad, thou may'st well be called Security, for thou takest
the safest course.   100
SECURITY
Faith, the quieter and the more contented, and, out of doubt,
the more godly; for merchants, in their courses, are never
pleased, but ever repining against heaven: one prays for a
westerly wind to carry his ship forth; another for an easterly
to bring his ship home; and at every shaking of a leaf he   105
falls into an agony to think what danger his ship is in on
such a coast, and so forth. The farmer, he is ever at odds
with the weather: sometimes the clouds have been too
barren; sometimes the heavens forget themselves, their
harvests answer not their hopes; sometimes the season falls   110
out too fruitful, corn will bear no price, and so forth. Th'
artificer, he's all for a stirring world; if his trade be too dull
and fall short of his expectation, then falls he out of joint.
Where we, that trade nothing but money, are free from all
this; we are pleased with all weathers: let it rain or hold up, 115
be calm or windy, let the season be whatsoever, let trade go
how it will, we take all in good part, e'en what please the
heavens to send us, so the sun stand not still, and the moon
keep her usual returns, and make up days, months, and
years—   120

112 *artificer* deviser, trickster (*O.E.D.*)
112 *dull* Ed. (full Q)
116 *calm* Qq (call me Q)

95 *thirty or forty.* By the 1571 Parliament, the interest rate was fixed at
   10 per cent.
113 *out of joint.* cf. *Hamlet* (I, v, 188): 'The time is out of joint'.

QUICKSILVER
And you have good security?

SECURITY
Ay, marry, Frank, that's the special point.

QUICKSILVER
And yet, forsooth, we must have trades to live withal; for
we cannot stand without legs, nor fly without wings (and
a number of such scurvy phrases). No, I say still, he that   125
has wit, let him live by his wit; he that has none, let him be
a tradesman.

SECURITY
Witty Master Francis! 'Tis pity any trade should dull that
quick brain of yours! Do but bring Knight Petronel into my
parchment toils once, and you shall never need to toil in any   130
trade, o' my credit! You know his wife's land?

QUICKSILVER
Even to a foot, sir; I have been often there; a pretty fine
seat, good land, all entire within itself.

SECURITY
Well wooded?

QUICKSILVER
Two hundred pounds' worth of wood ready to fell; and a   135
fine sweet house that stands just in the midst on't, like a
prick in the midst of a circle. Would I were your farmer, for
a hundred pound a year!

SECURITY
Excellent Master Francis, how I do long to do thee good!
'How I do hunger and thirst to have the honour to enrich   140
thee'! Ay, even to die that thou mightest inherit my living;
'even hunger and thirst'! For o' my religion, Master Francis—
and so tell Knight Petronel—I do it to do him a pleasure.

QUICKSILVER
Marry, Dad, his horses are now coming up to bear down his
lady; wilt thou lend him thy stable to set 'em in?   145

SECURITY
Faith, Master Francis, I would be loath to lend my stable

124 *we cannot stand without legs, nor fly without wings* proverbial.
  Tilley, F407
125 *scurvy* contemptible
130 *toils* traps

134–7 *Well-wooded? . . . circle.* Bawdy intention is clear.
137 *prick in the midst of a circle.* Bull's eye of a target, or the hole left by the
  compass point after proscribing a circle.

out of doors; in a greater matter I will pleasure him, but not
in this.

QUICKSILVER

A pox of your 'hunger and thirst'! Well, Dad, let him have
money; all he could any way get is bestowed on a ship now   150
bound for Virginia; the frame of which voyage is so closely
conveyed that his new lady nor any of her friends know it.
Notwithstanding, as soon as his lady's hand is gotten to the
sale of her inheritance, and you have furnished him with
money, he will instantly hoist sail and away.   155

SECURITY

Now, a frank gale of wind go with him, Master Frank! We
have too few such knight adventurers. Who would not sell
away competent certainties to purchase, with any danger,
excellent uncertainties? Your true knight venturer ever does
it. Let his wife seal today; he shall have his money today.   160

QUICKSILVER

Tomorrow, she shall, Dad, before she goes into the country.
To work her to which action with the more engines, I purpose presently to prefer my sweet Sin here to the place of
her gentlewoman; whom you (for the more credit) shall
present as your friend's daughter, a gentlewoman of the   165
country new come up with a will for awhile to learn fashions,
forsooth, and be toward some lady; and she shall buzz pretty
devices into her lady's ear, feeding her humours so service-
ably (as the manner of such as she is, you know)—

SECURITY

True, good Master Francis!   170

Enter SINDEFY

QUICKSILVER

That she shall keep her port open to anything she commends
to her.

SECURITY

O' my religion, a most fashionable project; as good she spoil
the lady, as the lady spoil her, for 'tis three to one of one
side. Sweet Mistress Sin, how are you bound to Master   175
Francis! I do not doubt to see you shortly wed one of the
head men of our City.

151 *frame* Ed. (fame Q)
151 *frame* plan
151–2 *closely conveyed* a closely guarded secret
160 *seal* set her seal
162 *engines* plans, plots, devices

SINDEFY

But, sweet Frank, when shall my father Security present me?

QUICKSILVER

With all festination; I have broken the ice to it already; and
will presently to the knight's house, whither, my good old   180
Dad, let me pray thee with all formality to man her.

SECURITY

Command me, Master Francis; 'I do hunger and thirst to do
thee service'. Come, sweet Mistress Sin, take leave of my
Winifred, and we will instantly meet frank Master Francis at
your lady's.   185

Enter WINIFRED *above*

WINIFRED

Where is my Cu there? Cu?

SECURITY

Ay, Winnie.

WINIFRED

Wilt thou come in, sweet Cu?

SECURITY

Ay, Winnie, presently!

Exeunt [all but QUICKSILVER]

QUICKSILVER

'Ay, Winnie', quod he! That's all he can do, poor man, he   190
may well cut off her name at Winnie. O 'tis an egregious
pander! What will not an usurous knave be, so he may be
rich? O 'tis a notable Jew's trump! I hope to live to see dog's
meat made of the old usurer's flesh, dice of his bones, and
indentures of his skin; and yet his skin is too thick to make   195
parchment, 'twould make good boots for a peterman to
catch salmon in. Your only smooth skin to make fine vellum
is your Puritan's skin; they be the smoothest and slickest
knaves in a country.

[Exit]

179 *festination* haste

193 *Jew's trump.* Earlier name for a Jew's harp; cant term for usurers.
196 *peterman.* A fisherman; from Peter boats, early trawlers.

[Act II, Scene iii

Before SIR PETRONEL'*s Lodging*]

Enter SIR PETRONEL *in boots, with a riding wand,*
[*followed by* QUICKSILVER]

PETRONEL

I'll out of this wicked town as fast as my horse can trot.
Here's now no good action for a man to spend his time in.
Taverns grow dead; ordinaries are blown up; plays are at a
stand; houses of hospitality at a fall; not a feather waving,
nor a spur jingling anywhere. I'll away instantly.   5

QUICKSILVER

Y'ad best take some crowns in your purse, Knight, or else
your eastward castle will smoke but miserably.

PETRONEL

O, Frank! My castle? Alas, all the castles I have are built
with air, thou know'st!

QUICKSILVER

I know it, Knight, and therefore wonder whither your lady   10
is going.

PETRONEL

Faith, to seek her fortune, I think. I said I had a castle and
land eastward, and eastward she will, without contradiction.
Her coach and the coach of the sun must meet full butt; and
the sun being outshined with her ladyship's glory, she fears   15
he goes westward to hang himself.

QUICKSILVER

And I fear, when her enchanted castle becomes invisible,
her ladyship will return and follow his example.

PETRONEL

O that she would have the grace, for I shall never be able to
pacify her, when she sees herself deceived so.   20

QUICKSILVER

As easily as can be. Tell her she mistook your directions, and
that shortly yourself will down with her to approve it; then
clothe but her crupper in a new gown, and you may drive

---

  1 s.d. *riding wan(d)* a switch
  1 *wand* ed. (*wan* Q)
 22 *approve* prove
 23 *crupper* hindquarters (usually of horse)

---

16 *westward to hang.* Another reference to Tyburn's gallows.

her any way you list. For these women, sir, are like Essex
calves, you must wriggle 'em on by the tail still, or they will   25
never drive orderly.

PETRONEL

But, alas, sweet Frank, thou know'st my hability will not
furnish her blood with those costly humours.

QUICKSILVER

Cast that cost on me, sir. I have spoken to my old pander,
Security, for money or commodity; and commodity (if   30
you will) I know he will procure you.

PETRONEL

Commodity! Alas, what commodity?

QUICKSILVER

Why, sir, what say you to figs and raisins?

PETRONEL

A plague of figs and raisins, and all such frail commodities!
We shall make nothing of 'em.   35

QUICKSILVER

Why, then, sir, what say you to forty pound in roasted beef?

PETRONEL

Out upon't! I have less stomach to that than to the figs and
raisins. I'll out of town, though I sojourn with a friend of
mine; for stay here I must not; my creditors have laid to
arrest me, and I have no friend under heaven but my sword   40
to bail me.

QUICKSILVER

God's me, Knight, put 'em in sufficient sureties, rather than
let your sword bail you! Let 'em take their choice, either the

27 *hability* ability
28 *humours* indulgences
34 *frail* play on the meaning frail: basket
42 *sureties* securities

24–5 *Essex calves.* According to Fuller's *The Worthies of England* (1672),
I, 320, these were proverbially 'the *fattest, fairest* and *finest flesh* in
England'. Proverbial. Tilley, C21.

30 *commodity.* A parcel of goods sold in credit by a usurer to a needy
person, who immediately raised some money by reselling them at a
lower price, generally to the usurer himself (*O.E.D.*).

40–1 *sword to bail me.* Defend himself only with his sword, or perhaps, enlist
in the army.

King's Bench or the Fleet, or which of the two Counters
they like best, for, by the Lord, I like none of 'em.   45

PETRONEL

Well, Frank, there is no jesting with my earnest necessity;
thou know'st if I make not present money to further my
voyage begun, all's lost, and all I have laid out about it.

QUICKSILVER

Why, then, sir, in earnest, if you can get your wise lady to set
her hand to the sale of her inheritance, the bloodhound,   50
Security, will smell out ready money for you instantly.

PETRONEL

There spake an angel! To bring her to which conformity, I
must feign myself extremely amorous; and alleging urgent
excuses for my stay behind, part with her as passionately as
she would from her foisting hound.   55

QUICKSILVER

You have the sow by the right ear, sir. I warrant there was
never child longed more to ride a cock-horse or wear his
new coat, than she longs to ride in her new coach. She would
long for everything when she was a maid; and now she will
run mad for 'em. I lay my life, she will have every year four   60
children; and what charge and change of humour you must
endure while she is with child; and how she will tie you to
your tackling till she be with child, a dog would not endure.

---

55 *foisting* farting
56 *sow by the . . . ear* proverbial. Tilley, S684

---

44 *King's Bench.* A debtors' prison.
44 *the Fleet.* A prison near Fleet ditch.
44 *the two Counters.* The two debtors' prisons of London, under control
   of the sheriff, were at Wood Street and at Poultry Street near St
   Mildred's Church. 'A man of means could live in comfort in either;
   indeed, for some people they served as a favourite retreat . . . An apart-
   ment on the Master's Side of the prison was the best accommodation
   provided. The Knight's Ward was not so good, but comfortable as
   prison usage went. The Twopenny Ward and the Hole were no better
   than common jails—in some respects worse, for prisoners could count
   on no public assistance of any value in the provision of food, and a
   penniless man might actually starve to death in the Hole if he failed to
   secure relief or help from one of the citizens' legacies or the Christmas-
   treat funds provided for the very poor'. Note 7 to 'The Counter's
   Commonwealth', in Judges, ed., op. cit., p. 518.
52 *angel.* Pun on a coin worth 7*s.* 6*d.* cf. *Volpone*, II, iv, 21.

Nay, there is no turnspit dog bound to his wheel more
servilely than you shall be to her wheel; for as that dog can   65
never climb the top of his wheel but when the top comes
under him, so shall you never climb the top of her contentment but when she is under you.

PETRONEL

'Slight, how thou terrifiest me!

QUICKSILVER

Nay, hark you, sir; what nurses, what midwives, what fools,   70
what physicians, what cunning women must be sought for
(fearing sometimes she is bewitched, sometimes in a con-
sumption) to tell her tales, to talk bawdy to her, to make her
laugh, to give her glisters, to let her blood under the tongue,
and betwixt the toes; how she will revile and kiss you, spit   75
in your face, and lick it off again; how she will vaunt you are
her creature; she made you of nothing; how she could have
had thousand-mark jointures; she could have been made a
lady by a Scotch knight, and never ha' married him; she
could have had poynados in her bed every morning; how she   80
set you up, and how she will pull you down: you'll never be
able to stand of your legs to ensure it.

PETRONEL

Out of my fortune! What a death is my life bound face to
face to! The best is, a large time-fitted conscience is bound
to nothing; marriage is but a form in the school of policy,   85
to which scholars sit fastened only with painted chains. Old
Security's young wife is ne'er the further off with me.

74 *glisters* clysters, enemas
78 *jointures* dowries
84 *large* liberal, bountiful
85 *policy* politically astute action

64–8 *Nay . . . under you.* Refers to the practice of harnessing dogs within
   a kind of treadwheel to turn meat on spits in the kitchens.
69 *'Slight.* Abbreviation for God's light, petty oath.
78 *mark.* English or Scottish coin worth 13*s*. 4*d*.
79 *Scotch knight.* In Scotland marriage was assumed after cohabitation—
   sharing a bed and board; consent could be sworn before witnesses
   other than magistrates, and providing copulation could be proved by
   witnesses or inferred 'by the circumstances ordinarily accompanying
   it', the marriage was legal.
80 *poynados.* Daggers (with phallic overtones); also panadas, a kind of
   medieval bread-pudding. cf. proverb. Tilley, P633: 'puddings and
   paramours would be hotly handled'.

QUICKSILVER

Thereby lies a tale, sir. The old usurer will be here instantly,
with my punk Sindefy, whom you know your lady has
promised me to entertain for her gentlewoman; and he (with   90
a purpose to feed on you) invites you most solemnly by me
to supper.

PETRONEL

It falls out excellently fitly: I see desire of gain makes
jealousy venturous.

Enter GERTRUDE

See, Frank, here comes my lady. Lord, how she views thee!   95
She knows thee not, I think, in this bravery.

GERTRUDE

How now? Who be you, I pray?

QUICKSILVER

One Master Francis Quicksilver, an't please your Ladyship.

GERTRUDE

God's my dignity! As I am a lady, if he did not make me
blush so that mine eyes stood a-water, would I were un-   100
married again! Where's my woman, I pray?

Enter SECURITY *and* SINDEFY

QUICKSILVER

See, Madam, she now comes to attend you.

SECURITY

God save my honourable Knight and his worshipful Lady!

GERTRUDE

Y'are very welcome; you must not put on your hat yet.

SECURITY

No, Madam; till I know your Ladyship's further pleasure,   105
I will not presume.

GERTRUDE

And is this a gentleman's daughter new come out of the
country?

90 *entertain* engage in service
96 *bravery* fine clothes

---

88 *Thereby lies a tale, sir.* cf. *The Merry Wives of Windsor* (I, iv, 159).
90–1 (*with . . . you*). Another echo of *Hamlet* (IV, iii, 19): 'Not where he
    eats but where he is eaten'.
94 *jealousy.* The first mention of Security's humour (melancholy).
104 *you must not put on your hat yet.* Here Security, who has gallantly
    removed his hat to observe a lady's entrance, is told hamfistedly to
    keep if off.

SECURITY

She is, Madam; and one that her father hath a special care
to bestow in some honourable lady's service, to put her out   110
of her honest humours, forsooth; for she had a great desire
to be a nun, an't please you.

GERTRUDE

A nun? What nun? A nun substantive, or a nun adjective?

SECURITY

A nun substantive, Madam, I hope, if a nun be a noun. But
I mean, Lady, a vowed maid of that order.   115

GERTRUDE

I'll teach her to be a maid of the order, I warrant you! And
can you do any work belongs to a lady's chamber?

SINDEFY

What I cannot do, Madam, I would be glad to learn.

GERTRUDE

Well said, hold up then; hold up your head, I say! Come
hither a little.   120

SINDEFY

I thank your Ladyship.

GERTRUDE

And hark you—good man, you may put on your hat now;
I do not look on you—I must have you of my faction now;
not of my knight's, maid!

SINDEFY

No, forsooth, Madam, of yours.   125

GERTRUDE

And draw all my servants in my bow, and keep my counsel,
and tell me tales, and put me riddles, and read on a book
sometimes when I am busy, and laugh at country gentle-
women, and command anything in the house for my retainers,
and care not what you spend, for it is all mine; and in any   130
case, be still a maid, whatsoever you do, or whatsoever any
man can do unto you.

SECURITY

I warrant your Ladyship for that.

GERTRUDE

Very well; you shall ride in my coach with me into the
country tomorrow morning. Come, Knight, pray thee, let's   135
make a short supper, and to bed presently.

---

126 *draw . . . in my bow.* Bend to my will, bring under control. Proverbial.
    Tilley, Y35.
131 *maid.* Possible pun on 'maid' = virgin and 'make' = sexual intercourse.

SECURITY

Nay, good Madam, this night I have a short supper at home
waits on his worship's acceptation.

GERTRUDE

By my faith, but he shall not go, sir; I shall swoon and he
sup from me.   140

PETRONEL

Pray thee, forbear; shall he lose his provision?

GERTRUDE

Ay, by'r Lady, sir, rather than I lose my longing. Come in,
I say—as I am a lady, you shall not go!

QUICKSILVER

[*Aside to* SECURITY] I told him what a bur he had gotten.

SECURITY

If you will not sup from your knight, Madam, let me entreat   145
your Ladyship to sup at my house with him.

GERTRUDE

No, by my faith, sir; then we cannot be abed soon enough
after supper.

PETRONEL

What a medicine is this! Well, Master Security, you are new
married as well as I; I hope you are bound as well. We must   150
honour our young wives, you know.

QUICKSILVER

[*Aside to* SECURITY] In policy, Dad, till tomorrow she has
sealed.

SECURITY

I hope in the morning, yet, your Knighthood will breakfast
with me?   155

PETRONEL

As early as you will, sir.

SECURITY

Thank your good worship; 'I do hunger and thirst to do you
good, sir'.

GERTRUDE

Come, sweet Knight, come, 'I do hunger and thirst to be abed
with thee'.   160

Exeunt

142 *by'r Lady* ed. (by lady Q)

Act III, Scene i

[SECURITY's *House*]

Enter PETRONEL, QUICKSILVER, SECURITY, BRAMBLE, *and*
WINIFRED

PETRONEL

Thanks for our feast-like breakfast, good Master Security;
I am sorry (by reason of my instant haste to so long a voyage
as Virginia) I am without means by any kind amends to show
how affectionately I take your kindness, and to confirm by
some worthy ceremony a perpetual league of friendship   5
betwixt us.

SECURITY

Excellent Knight, let this be a token betwixt us of inviolable
friendship: I am new married to this fair gentlewoman, you
know, and by my hope to make her fruitful, though I be
something in years, I vow faithfully unto you to make you   10
godfather (though in your absence) to the first child I am
blessed withal; and henceforth call me Gossip, I beseech
you, if you please to accept it.

PETRONEL

In the highest degree of gratitude, my most worthy Gossip;
for confirmation of which friendly title, let me entreat my   15
fair Gossip, your wife, here, to accept this diamond, and keep
it as my gift to her first child; wheresoever my fortune, in
event of my voyage, shall bestow me.

SECURITY

How now, my coy wedlock! Make you strange of so noble a
favour? Take it, I charge you, with all affection, and, by   20

---

3 *amends* requitals   19 *Make you strange* are you hesitant?

---

12 *Gossip*. Godfather: usually chosen for his spiritual affinity.
8–29 *I am . . . despatch it*. Closely parallels the source, Masuccio's *Il
Novellino*, XL (1476). See Parrott, II, 838: 'Genefra, a rich Catalan,
falls in love with Adriana, the young wife of Cosmo, a silver-smith of
Amalfi. To obtain his end Genefra cultivates Cosmo's friendship and
so far wins over the unsuspecting husband that he is invited to stand
godfather to the first child of the marriage (cf. *Eastward Ho!*, III, i,
8–18). Forced to leave Amalfi, Genefra plots to carry off the wife and
enlists Cosmo as his accomplice by deluding him with a false tale of his
purpose to elope with a boatman's wife (cf. *Eastward Ho!*, III, ii,
204–42). Cosmo gladly promises his aid (cf. *Eastward Ho!*, III, ii, 243–53)
[and] forces his own wife to give a farewell kiss to Genefra (cf. *Eastward
Ho!*, III, i, 19–22) . . . '

way of taking your leave, present boldly your lips to our
honourable gossip.

QUICKSILVER

[*Aside*] How venturous he is to him, and how jealous to
others!

PETRONEL

Long may this kind touch of our lips print in our hearts all   25
the forms of affection. And now my good Gossip, if the
writings be ready to which my wife should seal, let them be
brought this morning before she takes coach into the country,
and my kindness shall work her to despatch it.

SECURITY

The writings are ready, sir. My learned counsel here,   30
Master Bramble the lawyer, hath perused them; and within
this hour, I will bring the scrivener with them to your worshipful lady.

PETRONEL

Good Master Bramble, I will here take my leave of you,
then. God send you fortunate pleas, sir, and contentious   35
clients!

BRAMBLE

And you foreright winds, sir, and a fortunate voyage!

                                                              Exit

                        Enter a MESSENGER

MESSENGER

Sir Petronel, here are three or four gentlemen desire to speak
with you.

PETRONEL

What are they?   40

QUICKSILVER

They are your followers in this voyage, Knight, Captain
Seagull and his associates; I met them this morning, and
told them you would be here.

PETRONEL

Let them enter, I pray you; I know they long to be gone,
for their stay is dangerous.   45

            Enter SEAGULL, SCAPETHRIFT, *and* SPENDALL

SEAGULL

God save my honourable Colonel!

37 *foreright* favourable

PETRONEL

Welcome, good Captain Seagull and worthy gentlemen. If
you will meet my friend Frank here, and me, at the Blue
Anchor Tavern by Billingsgate this evening, we will there
drink to our happy voyage, be merry, and take boat to our   50
ship with all expedition.

SPENDALL

Defer it no longer, I beseech you, sir; but as your voyage is
hitherto carried closely, and in another knight's name, so for
your own safety and ours, let it be continued—our meeting
and speedy purpose of departing known to as few as is   55
possible, lest your ship and goods be attached.

QUICKSILVER

Well advised, Captain! Our colonel shall have money this
morning to despatch all our departures. Bring those gentlemen at night to the place appointed, and with our skins full
of vintage we'll take occasion by the 'vantage, and away.   60

SPENDALL

We will not fail but be there, sir.

PETRONEL

Good morrow, good Captain, and my worthy associates.
Health and all sovereignty to my beautiful Gossip. For you,
sir, we shall see you presently with the writings.

SECURITY

With writings and crowns to my honourable Gossip. 'I do   65
hunger and thirst to do you good, sir'!

Exeunt

Act III, Scene ii

[An Inn-yard]

Enter a COACHMAN *in haste, in's frock, feeding*

COACHMAN

Here's a stir when citizens ride out of town, indeed, as if all
the house were afire! 'Slight, they will not give a man leave
to eat's breakfast afore he rises!

Enter HAMLET, *a footman, in haste*

53 *carried closely* kept secret
56 *attached* apprehended by writ, arrested

52, 61 s.p. SPENDALL Ed. (*Spoyl.* Q) See note, *Dramatis Personae*, [17].
  3 s.d. *Enter* HAMLET. See note, *Dramatis Personae*, [18].

HAMLET

What, coachman! My lady's coach, for shame! Her Ladyship's ready to come down.   5

Enter POTKIN, *a tankard-bearer*

POTKIN

'Sfoot, Hamlet, are you mad? Whither run you now? You
should brush up my old mistress!

[*Exit* HAMLET]

Enter SINDEFY

SINDEFY

What, Potkin? You must put off your tankard, and put on
your blue coat and wait upon Mistress Touchstone into the
country.   *Exit*   10

POTKIN

I will, forsooth, presently.   *Exit*

Enter MISTRESS FOND *and* MISTRESS GAZER

FOND

Come, sweet Mistress Gazer, let's watch here, and see my
Lady Flash take coach.

GAZER

O' my word, here's a most fine place to stand in. Did you see
the new ship launched last day, Mistress Fond?   15

FOND

O God, and we citizens should lose such a sight!

GAZER

I warrant here will be double as many people to see her take
coach as there were to see it take water.

FOND

O, she's married to a most fine castle i' th' country, they
say.   20

GAZER

But there are no giants in the castle, are there?

FOND

O no; they say her knight killed 'em all, and therefore he was
knighted.

---

7 *brush up* brighten up, freshen
9 *blue coat* footman's livery

---

12 s.d. Mistresses Fond and Gazer typify the condescending attitude
towards city wives in many of the coterie, private theatre, plays.

GAZER
Would to God her Ladyship would come away!

Enter GERTRUDE, MISTRESS TOUCHSTONE, SINDEFY, HAMLET,
POTKIN

FOND
She comes, she comes, she comes!   25
GAZER ⎫
FOND ⎭
Pray heaven bless your Ladyship!
GERTRUDE
Thank you, good people! My coach! For the love of heaven,
my coach! In good truth I shall swoon else.
HAMLET
Coach, coach, my lady's coach!   *Exit*
GERTRUDE
As I am a lady, I think I am with child already, I long for a   30
coach so. May one be with child afore they are married,
mother?
MISTRESS TOUCHSTONE
Ay, by'r Lady, Madam; a little thing does that. I have seen a
little prick no bigger than a pin's head swell bigger and
bigger till it has come to an ancome; and e'en so 'tis in these   35
cases.

Enter HAMLET

HAMLET
Your coach is coming, Madam.
GERTRUDE
That's well said. Now, heaven! Methinks I am e'en up to the
knees in preferment!   [*Sings*]
    But a little higher, but a little higher, but a little higher;   40
    There, there, there lies Cupid's fire!
MISTRESS TOUCHSTONE
But must this young man, an't please you, Madam, run by
your coach all the way a-foot?
GERTRUDE
Ay, by my faith, I warrant him! He gives no other milk, as
I have another servant does.   45

---

35 *ancome.* Boil or swelling, rising unexpectedly.
40-1 *But a little higher* . . . The refrain of a song in Campion's *Book of Airs*
    (1601), entitled 'Mistress, Since You So Much Desire' (Fellowes ,op. cit.,
    Series I, 13, 59–60). A 1617 version, 'Beauty Since You So Much Desire'
    (Series 2, 11, 40–1), has the innuendo of Gertrude's lines.

MISTRESS TOUCHSTONE

Alas, 'tis e'en pity, methinks! For God's sake, Madam, buy
him but a hobby-horse; let the poor youth have something
betwixt his legs to ease 'em. Alas, we must do as we would
be done to!

GERTRUDE

Go to, hold your peace, dame; you talk like an old fool, I   50
tell you.

Enter PETRONEL *and* QUICKSILVER

PETRONEL

Wilt thou be gone, sweet honeysuckle, before I can go with
thee?

GERTRUDE

I pray thee, sweet Knight, let me; I do so long to dress up
thy castle afore thou com'st. But I marle how my modest   55
sister occupies herself this morning, that she cannot wait on
me to my coach, as well as her mother!

QUICKSILVER

Marry, Madam, she's married by this time to prentice
Golding. Your father, and some one more, stole to church
with 'em, in all the haste, that the cold meat left at your   60
wedding might scrve to furnish their nuptial table.

GERTRUDE

There's no base fellow, my father, now! But he's e'en fit to
father such a daughter: he must call me daughter no more
now; but 'Madam', and, 'please you Madam', and, 'please
your worship, Madam', indeed. Out upon him! Marry his   65
daughter to a base prentice!

MISTRESS TOUCHSTONE

What should one do? Is there no law for one that marries a
woman's daughter against her will? How shall we punish
him, Madam?

GERTRUDE

As I am a lady, an't would snow, we'd so pebble 'em with   70
snowballs as they come from church! But sirrah, Frank
Quicksilver—

QUICKSILVER

Ay, Madam.

55 *marle* marvel

4

GERTRUDE
Dost remember since thou and I clapped what-d'ye-call'ts
in the garret?   75
QUICKSILVER
I know not what you mean, Madam.
GERTRUDE   [*Sings*]
His head as white as milk,
All flaxen was his hair;
But now he is dead,
And laid in his bed,   80
And never will come again.
God be at your labour!

Enter TOUCHSTONE, GOLDING, MILDRED *with rosemary*

PETRONEL
[*Aside*] Was there ever such a lady?
QUICKSILVER
See, Madam, the bride and bridegroom!
GERTRUDE
God's my precious! God give you joy, Mistress What-lack-   85
you! Now out upon thee, baggage! My sister married in a
taffeta hat! Marry, hang you! Westward with a wanion t' ye!
Nay, I have done wi' ye, minion, then, i'faith; never look to
have my countenance any more, nor anything I can do for
thee. Thou ride in my coach? Or come down to my castle?   90
Fie upon thee! I charge thee in my Ladyship's name, call
me sister no more.
TOUCHSTONE
An't please your worship, this is not your sister; this is my
daughter, and she calls me father, and so does not your
Ladyship, an't please your worship, Madam.   95
MISTRESS TOUCHSTONE
No, nor she must not call thee father by heraldry, because

87 *wanion* plague or vengeance (*O.E.D.*)
94 *calls* Q2 (cal Q)

74–5 *clapped . . . garret.* None too subtle reference to sexual matters,
characteristic of the licentious Gertrude.
77–81 *His head*, etc. Parodies Ophelia's song in *Hamlet*, IV, v, 188–97.
For music see Chappell, op. cit., I, 237.
85–6 *Mistress What-lack-you.* Nick-name taken from the greeting of an
apprentice.

thou mak'st thy prentice thy son as well as she. Ah, thou mis-
proud prentice, dar'st thou presume to marry a lady's
sister?

GOLDING

It pleased my master, forsooth, to embolden me with his   100
favour; and though I confess myself far unworthy so worthy
a wife (being in part her servant, as I am your prentice) yet
(since I may say it without boasting) I am born a gentleman,
and by the trade I have learned of my master (which I trust
taints not my blood) able with mine own industry and   105
portion to maintain your daughter, my hope is, heaven will
so bless our humble beginning, that in the end I shall be no
disgrace to the grace with which my master hath bound me
his double prentice.

TOUCHSTONE

Master me no more, son, if thou think'st me worthy to be   110
thy father.

GERTRUDE

Sun? Now, good Lord, how he shines, and you mark him!
He's a gentleman?

GOLDING

Ay, indeed, Madam, a gentleman born.

PETRONEL

Never stand o' your gentry, Master Bridegroom; if your   115
legs be no better than your arms, you'll be able to stand upon
neither shortly.

TOUCHSTONE

An't please your good worship, sir, there are two sorts of
gentleman.

PETRONEL

What mean you, sir?   120

TOUCHSTONE

Bold to put off my hat to your worship—   [*Doffs his hat*]

PETRONEL

Nay, pray forbear, sir, and then forth with your two sorts
of gentlemen.

TOUCHSTONE

If your worship will have it so: I say there are two sorts of

116 *arms* coat of arms

---

112 *Sun.* The same pun is found in John Donne, 'Ascention', *Divine Poems*,
    ed. H. J. C. Grierson, *The Poems of John Donne* (London, 1939), p. 292.
    'Joy at the uprising of this Sunne, and Sonne'.

gentlemen. There is a gentleman artificial, and a gentleman   125
natural. Now, though your worship be a gentleman natural—
'work upon that now'!

QUICKSILVER
Well said old Touchstone; I am proud to hear thee enter a
set speech, i'faith! Forth, I beseech thee!

TOUCHSTONE
Cry you mercy, sir, your worship's a gentleman I do not   130
know. If you be one of my acquaintance, y'are very much
disguised, sir.

QUICKSILVER
Go to, old quipper! Forth with thy speech, I say!

TOUCHSTONE
What, sir, my speeches were ever in vain to your gracious
worship; and therefore, till I speak to you gallantry indeed,   135
I will save my breath for my broth anon. Come, my poor
son and daughter, let us hide ourselves in our poor humility,
and live safe. Ambition consumes itself with the very show.
'Work upon that now'!

[*Exeunt* TOUCHSTONE, GOLDING *and* MILDRED]

GERTRUDE
Let him go, let him go, for God's sake! Let him make his   140
prentice his son, for God's sake! Give away his daughter,
for God's sake! And when they come a-begging to us, for
God's sake, let's laugh at their good husbandry, for God's
sake! Farewell, sweet Knight, pray thee make haste after.

PETRONEL
What shall I say? I would not have thee go.   145

QUICKSILVER   [*Sings*]
    Now, O now, I must depart;
    Parting though it absence move—
This ditty, Knight, do I see in thy looks in capital letters.
    What a grief 'tis to depart,

130 *Cry you mercy* I beg your pardon
133 *quipper* argumentative person
135 *gallantry* fine language of fops

125–6 *gentleman natural.* Pun meaning a natural gentleman, and idiot.
130–1 *your worship's a gentleman I do not know.* If your worship's a gentleman I cannot tell.
146–52 *Now, O now,* etc. A corruption of a Dowland Song (E. H. Fellowes,
ed., *Dowland, First Book of Airs* (London, 1920), I, 22–4).
148 *capital letters.* With emphasis, touching on the topic of cuckoldry.

And leave the flower that has my heart!   150
My sweet lady, and alack for woe,
Why should we part so?
Tell truth, Knight, and shame all dissembling lovers; does
not your pain lie on that side?

PETRONEL
If it do, canst thou tell me how I may cure it?   155

QUICKSILVER
Excellent easily! Divide yourself in two halves, just by the
girdlestead; send one half with your lady, and keep the
tother yourself. Or else do as all true lovers do—part with
your heart, and leave your body behind. I have seen't done
a hundred times: 'tis as easy a matter for a lover to part   160
without a heart from his sweetheart, and he ne'er the worse,
as for a mouse to get from a trap and leave his tail behind
him. See, here comes the writings.

Enter SECURITY *with a* SCRIVENER

SECURITY
Good morrow to my worshipful Lady! I present your
Ladyship with this writing, to which if you please to set   165
your hand, with your knight's, a velvet gown shall attend
your journey, o' my credit.

GERTRUDE
What writing is it, Knight?

PETRONEL
The sale, sweetheart, of the poor tenement I told thee of,
only to make a little money to send thee down furniture for   170
my castle, to which my hand shall lead thee.

GERTRUDE
Very well! Now give me your pen, I pray.

QUICKSILVER
[*Aside*] It goes down without chewing, i'faith!

SCRIVENER
Your worships deliver this as your deed?

BOTH
We do.   175

GERTRUDE
So now, Knight, farewell till I see thee!

PETRONEL
All farewell to my sweetheart!

157 *girdlestead* waist
162 *his* ed. (her Q)
175 s.p. BOTH ed. (*Ambo.* Q)

MISTRESS TOUCHSTONE
Good-bye, son Knight!

PETRONEL
Farewell, my good mother!

GERTRUDE
Farewell, Frank; I would fain take thee down if I could.   180

QUICKSILVER
I thank your good Ladyship. Farewell, Mistress Sindefy.

Exeunt [GERTRUDE *and her party*]

PETRONEL
O tedious voyage, whereof there is no end! What will they
think of me?

QUICKSILVER
Think what they list. They longed for a vagary into the
country, and now they are fitted. So a woman marry to ride   185
in a coach, she cares not if she ride to her ruin. 'Tis the great
end of many of their marriages. This is not first time a lady
has rid a false journey in her coach, I hope.

PETRONEL
Nay, 'tis no matter. I care little what they think; he that
weighs men's thoughts has his hands full of nothing. A man,   190
in the course of this world, should be like a surgeon's instru-
ment: work in the wounds of others, and feel nothing himself—the sharper and subtler, the better.

QUICKSILVER
As it falls out now, Knight, you shall not need to devise
excuses, or endure her outcries, when she returns. We shall   195
now be gone before, where they cannot reach us.

PETRONEL
Well, my kind compeer, you have now th'assurance we both
can make you. Let me now entreat you, the money we agreed
on may be brought to the Blue Anchor, near to Billingsgate,

197 *compeer* gossip

180 *take thee down.* Travel with, or have sexual intercourse with.
187–8 *This is not first time*, etc. H. & S. note (incorrectly) that this passage
is paralleled in Field's *A Woman is a Weathercock* (II, iv, D3ᵛ). (It is
found in Field's *Amends for Ladies*, II, iv, 32.) Nevertheless, this
confirms Peery's hypothesis that Field played the part of Quicksilver.
(See note, I, i, 132.)
199 *Blue Anchor.* Tavern mentioned in *The Roxburghe Ballads*, 1607.
199 *Billingsgate.* A river-gate, wharf, and fish-market, on the Thames a
little below London Bridge. The great market-place of seventeenth-
century London.

by six o'clock; where I and my chief friends, bound for this   200
voyage, will with feasts attend you.

SECURITY

The money, my most honourable compeer, shall without
fail observe your appointed hour.

PETRONEL

Thanks, my dear Gossip, I must now impart
To your approved love a loving secret,   205
As one on whom my life doth more rely
In friendly trust than any man alive.
Nor shall you be the chosen secretary
Of my affections for affection only:
For if I protest (if God bless my return)   210
To make you partner in my actions' gain
As deeply as if you had ventured with me
Half my expenses. Know then, honest Gossip,
I have enjoyed with such divine contentment
A gentlewoman's bed, whom you well know,   215
That I shall ne'er enjoy this tedious voyage,
Nor live the least part of the time it asketh,
Without her presence; 'so I thirst and hunger'
To taste the dear feast of her company.
And if the hunger and the thirst you vow,   220
(As my sworn gossip) to my wished good
Be (as I know it is) unfeigned and firm,
Do me an easy favour in your power.

SECURITY

Be sure, brave Gossip, all that I can do,
To my best nerve, is wholly at your service: 225
Who is the woman, first, that is your friend?

PETRONEL

The woman is your learned counsel's wife,
The lawyer, Master Bramble; whom would you
Bring out this even', in honest neighbourhood,
To take his leave with you, of me your gossip.   230
I, in the meantime, will send this my friend
Home to his house, to bring his wife disguised,
Before his face, into our company;
For love hath made her look for such a wile
To free her from his tyrannous jealousy.   235
And I would take this course before another,
In stealing her away to make us sport
And gull his circumspection the more grossly.
And I am sure that no man like yourself

Hath credit with him to entice his jealousy   240
To so long stay abroad as may give time
To her enlargement in such safe disguise.
SECURITY
A pretty, pithy, and most pleasant project!
Who would not strain a point of neighbourhood,
For such a point-device, that, as the ship   245
Of famous Draco went about the world,
Will wind about the lawyer, compassing
The world himself; he hath it in his arms,
And that's enough, for him, without his wife.
A lawyer is ambitious, and his head   250
Cannot be praised nor raised too high,
With any fork of highest knavery.
I'll go fetch him straight.

                                        Exit SECURITY
PETRONEL
So, so. Now, Frank, go thou home to his house,
'Stead of his lawyer's, and bring his wife hither,   255
Who, just like to the lawyer's wife, is prisoned
With his stern usurous jealousy, which could never
Be over-reached thus, but with over-reaching.

                            Enter SECURITY
SECURITY
And, Master Francis, watch you th'instant time
To enter with his exit; 'twill be rare,   260
Two fine horned beasts—a camel and a lawyer!   [*Exit*]
QUICKSILVER
How the old villain joys in villainy!

                            Enter SECURITY
SECURITY
And hark you, Gossip, when you have her here,

---

242 *enlargement* freedom of action
253 *him* Ed. (her Q)
257 *his* Qq (eis Q)
261 *Two fine* Qq (To finde Q)

---

245 *point-device.* Pun meaning (1) a point of vice and (2) the best way
    imaginable.
246 *Draco.* Drake's ship at Deptford.
261 *a camel and a lawyer.* Camel; thought to be a horned beast. Frequently
    used by Chapman in the context of cuckoldry. See H. & S., IX, 642.

Have your boat ready; ship her to your ship
With utmost haste, lest Master Bramble stay you.   265
To o'er-reach that head that out-reacheth all heads,
'Tis a trick rampant! 'Tis a very quiblin!
I hope this harvest to pitch cart with lawyers,
Their heads will be so forked. 'This sly touch
Will get apes to invent a number such'.   *Exit*   270
QUICKSILVER
Was ever rascal honeyed so with poison?
'He that delights in slavish avarice,
Is apt to joy in every sort of vice'.
Well, I'll go fetch his wife, whilst he the lawyer.
PETRONEL
But stay, Frank, let's think how we may disguise her   275
Upon this sudden.
QUICKSILVER
God's me, there's the mischief!
But hark you, here's an excellent device;
'Fore God, a rare one! I will carry her
A sailor's gown and cap, and cover her,   280
And a player's beard.
PETRONEL
And what upon her head?
QUICKSILVER
I tell you; a sailor's cap! 'Slight, God forgive me,
What kind of figent memory have you?
PETRONEL
Nay, then, what kind of figent wit hast thou?   285
A sailor's cap? How shall she put it off
When thou present'st her to our company?
QUICKSILVER
Tush, man! For that, make her a saucy sailor.
PETRONEL
Tush, tush, 'tis no fit sauce for such sweet mutton!
I know not what t'advise.   290

267 *rampant* spirited   267 *quiblin* a pun, a trick
270 *apes* imitators, actors
274 *lawyer* Ed. (lawyers Q)
275–84 prose Q
284 *figent* restless, fidgety
289–90 prose Q

289 *mutton.* From the proverb 'sweet meat must have a sour sauce'; Tilley,
    M839. Also mutton: prostitute.

Enter SECURITY, *with his wife's gown*

SECURITY
Knight, Knight, a rare device!
PETRONEL
'Swounds, yet again!
QUICKSILVER
What stratagem have you now?
SECURITY
The best that ever! You talked of disguising?
PETRONEL
Ay, marry, Gossip, that's our present care.   295
SECURITY
Cast care away then; here's the best device
For plain security (for I am no better),
I think, that ever lived. Here's my wife's gown,
Which you may put upon the lawyer's wife,
And which I brought you, sir, for two great reasons: 300
One is, that Master Bramble may take hold
Of some suspicion that it is my wife,
And gird me so, perhaps, with his law wit;
The other (which is policy indeed)
Is, that my wife may now be tied at home,   305
Having no more but her old gown abroad,
And not show me a quirk, while I firk others.
Is not this rare?
BOTH
The best that ever was!
SECURITY
Am I not born to furnish gentlemen?   310
PETRONEL
O my dear Gossip!
SECURITY
Well, hold, Master Francis!
Watch when the lawyer's out, and put it in.
And now I will go fetch him.   *Exit*
QUICKSILVER
O my Dad!   315

292 *'Swounds* God's wounds
307 *quirk* sudden turn
308 s.p. BOTH ed. (*Ambo.* Q)
312–15 prose Q

307 *firk*. Bedevil. (Security here resembles Vice of the Mystery Play.)

He goes, as 'twere the devil, to fetch the lawyer;
And devil shall he be, if horns will make him.

[*Re-enter* SECURITY]

PETRONEL
Why, how now, Gossip? Why stay you there musing?
SECURITY
A toy, a toy runs in my head, i'faith!
QUICKSILVER
A pox of that head! Is there more toys yet?   320
PETRONEL
What is it, pray thee, Gossip?
SECURITY
Why, sir, what if you
Should slip away now with my wife's best gown,
I have no security for it?
QUICKSILVER
For that, I hope, Dad, you will take our words.   325
SECURITY
Ay, by th'mass, your word! That's a proper staff
For wise Security to lean upon!
But 'tis no matter, once I'll trust my name
On your cracked credits; let it take no shame.
Fetch the wench, Frank!   *Exit* 330
QUICKSILVER
I'll wait upon you, sir,
And fetch you over, you were ne'er so fetched.
Go to the tavern, Knight; your followers
Dare not be drunk, I think, before their captain.   *Exit*
PETRONEL
Would I might lead them to no hotter service,   335
Till our Virginian gold were in our purses!   *Exit*

316 *to fetch* also to trick, gull
316–24 prose Q
319 *toy* prank
335 *them* Qq (then Q)

316 *He goes . . . lawyer.* cf. Chaucer's *Friar's Tale*, where the devil carries
off the lawyer because the villagers mean it literally when they say,
'Devil take you!' Typical of Chapman's habit of matter-of-fact citing
of obscure allusions.

[Act III, Scene iii

Blue Anchor Tavern, Billingsgate]

Enter SEAGULL, SPENDALL, *and* SCAPETHRIFT, *in the tavern,*
with a DRAWER

SEAGULL

Come, drawer, pierce your neatest hogsheads, and let's have
cheer, not fit for your Billingsgate tavern, but for our
Virginian colonel; he will be here instantly.

DRAWER

You shall have all things fit, sir; please you have any more
wine?   5

SPENDALL

More wine, slave! Whether we drink it or no, spill it, and
draw more.

SCAPETHRIFT

Fill all the pots in your house with all sorts of liquor, and
let 'em wait on us here like soldiers in their pewter coats;
and though we do not employ them now, yet we will main-   10
tain 'em till we do.

DRAWER

Said like an honourable captain! You shall have all you can
command, sir!   *Exit* DRAWER

SEAGULL

Come, boys, Virginia longs till we share the rest of her
maidenhead.   15

SPENDALL

Why, is she inhabited already with any English?

SEAGULL

A whole country of English is there, man, bred of those that
were left there in '79. They have married with the Indians,
and make 'em bring forth as beautiful faces as any we have
in England; and therefore the Indians are so in love with 'em,   20
that all the treasure they have they lay at their feet.

SCAPETHRIFT

But is there such treasure there, Captain, as I have heard?

9 *pewter coats* armour

18 *'79*. Grenville's earliest expedition to Virginia was in 1585 (Hakluyt,
Voyages, 1600, VIII, 310). Schelling upholds Edward Channing's
suggestion that the text refers to the 1587 expedition, known as 'the
lost colony', because some of the survivors apparently remained with
the Indians of Pamlico Sound.

SEAGULL

I tell thee, gold is more plentiful there than copper is with
us; and for as much red copper as I can bring, I'll have thrice
the weight in gold. Why, man, all their dripping-pans and   25
their chamber-pots are pure gold; and all the chains with
which they chain up their streets are massy gold; all the
prisoners they take are fettered in gold; and for rubies and
diamonds, they go forth on holidays and gather 'em by the
seashore to hang on their children's coats, and stick in their   30
caps, as commonly as our children wear saffron-gilt brooches,
and groats with holes in 'em.

SCAPETHRIFT

And is it a pleasant country withal?

SEAGULL

As ever the sun shined on; temperate and full of all sorts
of excellent viands; wild boar is as common there as our   35
tamest bacon is here; venison, as mutton. And then you
shall live freely there, without sergeants, or courtiers, or
lawyers, or intelligencers; only a few industrious Scots,
perhaps, who indeed arc dispersed over the face of the whole
earth. But as for them, there are no greater friends to   40
Englishmen and England, when they are out on't, in the
world, than they are. And for my part, I would a hundred
thousand of 'em were there; for we are all one countrymen
now, ye know; and we should find ten times more comfort
of them there than we do here. Then for your means to   45
advancement, there it is simple and not preposterously mixed.

---

38 *intelligencers* informers, spies

24–5 *red copper . . . gold.* 'Copper carrieth the price of all, so it be red', . . .
  'Our copper is better than theirs: and the reason is for that it is redder
  and harder . . .' written about the Virginian Indians, and 'copper . . . they
  esteem more than gold, which for the colour they make no account of',
  of the Florida Indians. *Hakluyt's Principal Voyages* (1600), The Hakluyt
  Society Extra Series, 12 vols. (Glasgow, 1904), VIII, 320, 329, 433.
  (Quoted first A. H. Gilbert, *MLN*, XXXIII (1918), 183–4; and H. & S.,
  IX, 663.)

25–32 *Why, man, all their dripping-pans,* etc. Closely parallels Sir Thomas
  More's *Utopia.* Sir Thomas More, *Utopia*, Book II, eds. E. Surtz &
  J. Hexter (New Haven, 1965), 153.

32 *groats.* Coin worth 4*d.* when minted in 1531–32. By 1600 slang for any
  small coin.

38–45 *only . . . here.* The famous gibe which was cancelled in all but two
  existing copies of Q.

You may be an alderman there, and never be scavenger;
you may be a nobleman, and never be a slave; you may
come to preferment enough, and never be a pander; to riches
and fortune enough, and have never the more villainy nor   50
the less wit.

SPENDALL
God's me! And how far is it thither?

SEAGULL
Some six weeks' sail, no more, with any indifferent good
wind. And if I get to any part of the coast of Africa, I'll sail
thither with any wind; or when I come to Cape Finisterre,   55
there's a foreright wind continually wafts us till we come at
Virginia. See, our colonel's come.

Enter SIR PETRONEL *with his followers*

PETRONEL
Well met, good Captain Seagull, and my noble gentlemen!
Now the sweet hour of our freedom is at hand. Come,
drawer, fill us some carouses, and prepare us for the mirth   60
that will be occasioned presently. Here will be a pretty
wench, gentlemen, that will bear us company all our voyage.

SEAGULL
Whatsoever she be, here's to her health, noble Colonel, both
with cap and knee.

PETRONEL
Thanks, kind Captain Seagull! She's one I love dearly, and   65
must not be known till we be free from all that know us.
And so, gentlemen, here's to her health!

BOTH
Let it come, worthy Colonel; 'we do hunger and thirst for it'!

53 *indifferent* moderately
58 s.d. PETRONEL *with his followers* Qq (*Petronell* Q)
68 s.p. BOTH ed. (*Ambo.* Q)

---

47 *scavenger*. Officer whose job it was to employ and supervise the poor to
keep the streets clean.
48 Here, 'You may be a nobleman, and never be a slave;' was changed to
the innocuous 'You may be any other officer, . . .'. A passage was
inserted at the end to fill the gap left by the removal of 38–45: 'Besides,
there we shall have no more law than conscience, and not too much of
either; serve God enough, eat and drink enough, and "enough is as
good as a feast" '. Adams believes the last if not all the corrections were
made by the printer (see above, *Note on the Text*, pp. xliif) and on the
basis of the facile proverb thrown in as a stop-gap, I would tend to
agree. See Adams, op. cit., pp. 163-9.
55 *Cape Finisterre*. The most westerly headland of Spain.

PETRONEL

Afore heaven, you have hit the phrase of one that her
presence will touch from the foot to the forehead, if ye knew   70
it.

SPENDALL

Why, then, we will join his forehead with her health, sir;
and, Captain Scapethrift, here's to 'em both!

[All kneel and drink]

Enter SECURITY *and* BRAMBLE

SECURITY

See, see, Master Bramble, 'fore heaven, their voyage cannot
but prosper: they are o' their knees for success to it.   75

BRAMBLE

And they pray to god Bacchus.

SECURITY

God save my brave Colonel, with all his tall captains and
corporals! See, sir, my worshipful learned counsel, Master
Bramble, is come to take his leave of you.

PETRONEL

Worshipful Master Bramble, how far do you draw us into   80
the sweet brier of your kindness! Come, Captain Seagull,
another health to this rare Bramble, that hath never a prick
about him.

SEAGULL

I pledge his most smooth disposition, sir. Come, Master
Security, bend your supporters, and pledge this notorious   85
health here.

SECURITY

Bend you yours likewise, Master Bramble; for it is you shall
pledge me.

SEAGULL

Not so, Master Security! He must not pledge his own
health!   90

SECURITY

No, Master Captain?

Enter QUICKSILVER *with* WINIFRED *disguised*

Why then, here's one is fitly come to do him that honour.

QUICKSILVER

Here's the gentlewoman your cousin, sir, whom, with much

84 s.p. SEAGULL Qq (*Pet.* Q)

74–131 *See, see, . . . lady.* The jesting of the deluded husband at his own
    expense and his misconstruing of his wife's fears derives from
    Masuccio XL. See Parrott, op. cit., p. 838.

entreaty, I have brought to take her leave of you in a
tavern; ashamed whereof, you must pardon her if she put   95
not off her mask.

PETRONEL
Pardon me, sweet cousin; my kind desire to see you before
I went, made me so importunate to entreat your presence
here.

SECURITY
How now, Master Francis, have you honoured this presence   100
with a fair gentlewoman?

QUICKSILVER
Pray, sir, take you no notice of her, for she will not be known
to you.

SECURITY
But my learned counsel, Master Bramble here, I hope may
know her.   105

QUICKSILVER
No more than you, sir, at this time; his learning must
pardon her.

SECURITY
Well, God pardon her for my part, and I do, I'll be sworn;
and so, Master Francis, here's to all that are going eastward
tonight, towards Cuckold's Haven; and so, to the health   110
of Master Bramble!

QUICKSILVER
[*Kneels*] I pledge it, sir. Hath it gone round, Captains?

SEAGULL
It has, sweet Frank; and the round closes with thee.

QUICKSILVER
Well, sir, here's to all eastward and toward cuckolds, and so
to famous Cuckold's Haven, so fatally remembered.   115

Surgit

PETRONEL
[*To* WINIFRED] Nay, pray thee, coz, weep not. Gossip
Security?

SECURITY
Ay, my brave Gossip.

PETRONEL
A word, I beseech you, sir. Our friend, Mistress Bramble
here, is so dissolved in tears that she drowns the whole   120
mirth of our meeting. Sweet Gossip, take her aside and
comfort her.

116 s.d. *Surgit* stands up

SECURITY

[*Aside to* WINIFRED] Pity of all true love, Mistress Bramble!
What, weep you to enjoy your love? What's the cause, lady?
Is't because your husband is so near, and your heart earns,　125
to have a little abused him? Alas, alas, the offence is too
common to be respected. So great a grace hath seldom
chanced to so unthankful a woman: to be rid of an old
jealous dotard, to enjoy the arms of a loving young knight,
that, when your prickless Bramble is withered with grief of　130
your loss, will make you flourish afresh in the bed of a lady.

Enter DRAWER

DRAWER

Sir Petronel, here's one of your watermen come to tell you
it will be flood these three hours; and that 'twill be dangerous
going against the tide, for the sky is overcast, and there was
a porcpisce even now seen at London Bridge, which is　135
always the messenger of tempests, he says.

PETRONEL

A porcpisce! What's that to th' purpose? Charge him, if he
love his life, to attend us; can we not reach Blackwall (where
my ship lies) against the tide, and in spite of tempests?
Captains and gentlemen, we'll begin a new ceremony at the　140
beginning of our voyage, which I believe will be followed
of all future adventurers.

SEAGULL

What's that, good Colonel?

PETRONEL

This, Captain Seagull. We'll have our provided supper
brought aboard Sir Francis Drake's ship, that hath com-　145
passed the world; where, with full cups and banquets, we
will do sacrifice for a prosperous voyage. My mind gives me
that some good spirits of the waters should haunt the desert
ribs of her, and be auspicious to all that honour her memory,
and will with like orgies enter their voyages.　150

---

125 *earns* feels keen grief

---

137 *porcpisce.* Jonson's spelling (see *Volpone*, II, i, 40). Stow's *Chronicle*
(*Annals*, p. 880, ed. 1615) tells of the appearance of a porpoise on the
Thames. The date recorded for the capture of a porpoise at West Ham
is 19 January 1606, but it must have been seen on the river before this
if *Volpone* was written late in 1605.
138 *Blackwall.* A mooring for merchant-ships, on the Thames below
London. (See Appendix 1 for location.)

SEAGULL

Rarely conceited! One health more to this motion, and aboard to perform it. He that will not this night be drunk, may he never be sober!

They compass in WINIFRED, *dance the drunken round, and drink carouses*

BRAMBLE

Sir Petronel and his honourable Captains, in these young services we old servitors may be spared. We only came to   155
take our leaves, and with one health to you all, I'll be bold to do so. Here, neighbour Security, to the health of Sir Petronel and all his captains!

SECURITY

You must bend, then, Master Bramble. [*They kneel*] So, now I am for you. I have one corner of my brain, I hope, fit to   160
bear one carouse more. Here, lady, to you that are encompassed there, and are ashamed of our company! Ha, ha, ha! By my troth, my learned counsel, Master Bramble, my mind runs so of Cuckold's Haven tonight, that my head runs over with admiration.   165

BRAMBLE

[*Aside*] But is not that your wife, neighbour?

SECURITY

[*Aside*] No, by my troth, Master Bramble. Ha, ha, ha! A pox of all Cuckold's Havens, I say!

BRAMBLE

[*Aside*] O' my faith, her garments are exceeding like your wife's.   170

SECURITY

[*Aside*] *Cucullus non facit monachum,* my learned counsel; all are not cuckolds that seem so, nor all seem not that are so. Give me your hand, my learned counsel; you and I will sup somewhere else than at Sir Francis Drake's ship tonight. Adieu, my noble Gossip!   175

BRAMBLE

Good fortune, brave Captains; fair skies God send ye!

ALL

Farewell, my hearts, farewell!

177 s.p. ALL ed. (*Omnes* Q)

---

171 *Cucullus non facit monachum.* The cowl does not make the monk, with a play on 'cuckold'. cf. *Twelfth Night*, I, v, 62.

PETRONEL

Gossip, laugh no more at Cuckold's Haven, Gossip.

SECURITY

I have done, I have done, sir. Will you lead, Master Bramble?
Ha, ha, ha!   *Exit [with* BRAMBLE]   180

PETRONEL

Captain Seagull, charge a boat!

ALL

A boat, a boat, a boat!   *Exeunt*

DRAWER

Y'are in a proper taking, indeed, to take a boat, especially at
this time of night, and against tide and tempest. They say
yet, 'drunken men never take harm'. This night will try the   185
truth of that proverb.   *Exit*

[Act III, Scene iv

Outside SECURITY'*s House*]

Enter SECURITY

SECURITY

What, Winnie? Wife, I say? Out of doors at this time! Where
should I seek the gad-fly? Billingsgate, Billingsgate, Billingsgate! She's gone with the knight, she's gone with the knight!
Woe be to thee, Billingsgate. A boat, a boat, a boat! A full
hundred marks for a boat!   *Exit*   5

---

180 *Exit* Qq (omitted in Q)
181 *charge* order
182 s.p. ALL ed. (*Omnes* Q)
183 *taking* state
185 *drunken men never take harm* proverbial. Tilley, M94

4–5 *A boat*, etc. Parody on *Richard III*, V, iv, 7, 13. Marston also parodies
      this passage in *The Scourge of Villainy*, Satire VII, i, *Parasiter*, V, i, and
      What you Will, II, i.

Act IV, Scene i

Enter SLITGUT, *with a pair of ox-horns, discovering Cuckold's*
Haven, above [*right*]

SLITGUT

All hail, fair haven of married men only, for there are none
but married men cuckolds! For my part, I presume not to
arrive here, but in my master's behalf (a poor butcher of
Eastcheap), who sends me to set up (in honour of Saint
Luke) these necessary ensigns of his homage. And up I got   5
this morning, thus early, to get up to the top of this famous
tree, that is all fruit and no leaves, to advance this crest of
my master's occupation. Up then; heaven and Saint Luke
bless me, that I be not blown into the Thames as I climb,
with this furious tempest. 'Slight, I think the devil be   10
abroad, in likeness of a storm, to rob me of my horns! Hark
how he roars! Lord, what a coil the Thames keeps! She
bears some unjust burden, I believe, that she kicks and
curvets thus to cast it. Heaven bless all honest passengers
that are upon her back now; for the bit is out of her mouth,   15
I see, and she will run away with 'em! So, so, I think I have
made it look the right way; it runs against London Bridge,
as it were, even full butt. And now, let me discover from this
lofty prospect, what pranks the rude Thames plays in her
desperate lunacy. O me, here's a boat has been cast away   20
hard by! Alas, alas, see one of her passengers, labouring for
his life to land at this haven here! Pray heaven he may
recover it! His next land is even just under me; hold out yet
a little, whatsoever thou art: pray, and take a good heart to
thee. 'Tis a man; take a man's heart to thee; yet a little   25

7 *tree* pole
12 *coil* turmoil
23 *recover* regain
23 *next* nearest

1 s.d. *Cuckold's Haven.* A point on the Surrey side of the Thames about
a mile below Rotherhithe Church (see Appendix 1). According to legend
the point had once been the site of a Temple of Fortune which was
later destroyed by fire. It was traditional on St Luke's day, 18 October,
for a butcher of Eastcheap to commemorate King John's cuckolding
of a miller, by erecting a pair of horns on a pole there. The cuckold
symbol is thus ambiguous since it is also the Christian emblem of
St Luke. cf. Breton, *Pasquil's Nightcap* (1612), G1ᵛ–H3ʳ.
4–5 *Saint Luke.* See above, s.d.

further, get up o' thy legs, man; now 'tis shallow enough.
So, so, so! Alas, he's down again! Hold thy wind, father!
'Tis a man in a night-cap. So! Now he's got up again; now
he's past the worst; yet, thanks be to heaven, he comes
toward me pretty and strongly.   30

Enter SECURITY *without his hat, in a nightcap, wet band, &c.*
                                            [*stage right*]

SECURITY
Heaven, I beseech thee, how have I offended thee! Where
am I cast ashore now, that I may go a righter way home by
land? Let me see. O, I am scarce able to look about me!
Where is there any sea-mark that I am acquainted withal?

SLITGUT
Look up, father; are you acquainted with this mark?   35

SECURITY
What! Landed at Cuckold's Haven! Hell and damnation! I
will run back and drown myself.
                                            He falls down

SLITGUT
Poor man, how weak he is! The weak water has washed
away his strength.

SECURITY
Landed at Cuckold's Haven! If it had not been to die twenty   40
times alive, I should never have 'scaped death! I will never
arise more; I will grovel here and eat dirt till I be choked. I
will make the gentle earth do that which the cruel water has
denied me!

SLITGUT
Alas, good father, be not so desperate! Rise, man; if you   45
will, I'll come presently and lead you home.

SECURITY
Home! Shall I make any know my home, that has known me
thus abroad? How low shall I crouch away, that no eye may
see me? I will creep on the earth while I live, and never look
heaven in the face more.   *Exit creeping*   50

34 *sea-mark* landmark
50 s.d. *creeping* Ed. (*creep* Q)

---

31 s.d. *band.* The collar which superseded the ruff.
42–50 *I will grovel here . . . face more.* Security is consistently shown to be
  of a melancholic humour, whose element is earth. His affinity to the
  earth here is not unnatural; and his exit creeping tallies with earlier
  hints at his satanic character. cf. the devil of the York Mystery Play
  who exits crawling.

SLITGUT

What young planet reigns now, trow, that old men are so
foolish? What desperate young swaggerer would have been
abroad such a weather as this upon the water? Ay me, see
another remnant of this unfortunate shipwreck, or some
other! A woman, i'faith, a woman! Though it be almost at   55
Saint Katherine's, I discern it to be a woman, for all her
body is above the water, and her clothes swim about her
most handsomely. O, they bear her up most bravely! Has
not a woman reason to love the taking up of her clothes the
better while she lives, for this? Alas, how busy the rude   60
Thames is about her! A pox o' that wave! It will drown her,
i'faith, 'twill drown her! Cry God mercy, she has 'scaped it,
I thank heaven she has 'scaped it! O, how she swims like a
mermaid! Some vigilant body look out and save her. That's
well said; just where the priest fell in, there's one sets down   65
a ladder, and goes to take her up. God's blessing o' thy heart,
boy! Now, take her up in thy arms and to bed with her.
She's up, she's up! She's a beautiful woman, I warrant her;
the billows durst not devour her.

Enter the DRAWER *in the Tavern before, with* WINIFRED
[*stage left*]

DRAWER

How fare you now, lady?   70

WINIFRED

Much better, my good friend, than I wish; as one desperate
of her fame, now my life is preserved.

DRAWER

Comfort yourself: that power that preserved you from death

---

51 *trow* pray
65 *well said* well done

---

51 *young planet*. Probably the new star discovered by Kepler on 17 October
    1604. '[It] had burst out in the constellation Serpentarius, and . . . sur-
    passed Jupiter in brightness'. E. B. Knobel, *Shakespeare's England*,
    2 vols. (Oxford, 1916), I, 455. cf. *Volpone*, II, i, 37.
57–8 *her clothes swim* . . . Perhaps another hit at *Hamlet*, IV, vii, 176–7.
    'Her clothes spread wide,/And mermaid-like awhile they bore her up'.
65 *just where the priest fell in*. See John Taylor, the Water Poet, *A Discovery
    by Sea from London to Salisbury*, Spencer Soc., reprint, London, 1869,
    p. 21: 'Down by St. Katherine's where the priest fell in', and Jonson's
    Masque of Augurs, 'We shew th'yron Gate,/The wheele of St. Kate,/And
    the place where the Priest fel in'. (H. & S., VII, 636, l. 201).

can likewise defend you from infamy, howsoever you
deserve it. Were not you one that took boat late this night   75
with a knight and other gentlemen at Billingsgate?

WINIFRED
Unhappy that I am, I was.

DRAWER
I am glad it was my good hap to come down thus far after
you, to a house of my friend's here in St. Katherine's; since
I am now happily made a mean to your rescue from the   80
ruthless tempest, which (when you took boat) was so
extreme, and the gentleman that brought you forth so desperate and unsober, that I feared long ere this I should hear
of your shipwreck, and therefore (with little other reason)
made thus far this way. And this I must tell you, since per-   85
haps you may make use of it: there was left behind you at
our tavern, brought by a porter (hired by the young gentleman that brought you) a gentlewoman's gown, hat, stockings,
and shoes; which, if they be yours, and you please to shift
you, taking a hard bed here in this house of my friend, I will   90
presently go fetch you.

WINIFRED
Thanks, my good friend, for your more than good news.
The gown with all things bound with it are mine; which if
you please to fetch as you have promised, I will boldly
receive the kind favour you have offered till your return;   95
entreating you, by all the good you have done in preserving
me hitherto, to let none take knowledge of what favour you
do me, or where such a one as I am bestowed, lest you incur
me much more damage in my fame than you have done me
pleasure in preserving my life.   100

DRAWER
Come in, lady, and shift yourself; resolve that nothing but
your own pleasure shall be used in your discovery.

WINIFRED
Thank you, good friend. The time may come, I shall requite
you.   *Exeunt*

SLITGUT
See, see, see! I hold my life, there's some other a-taking up   10

89–90 *shift you* change into a new suit of clothes

---

79 *St. Katherine's.* A reformatory for fallen women.

at Wapping now! Look, what a sort of people cluster about
the gallows there! In good troth, it is so. O me, a fine young
gentleman! What, and taken up at the gallows? Heaven
grant he be not one day taken down there! O' my life, it is
ominous! Well, he is delivered for the time. I see the people   110
have all left him; yet will I keep my prospect awhile, to see
if any more have been shipwrecked.

Enter QUICKSILVER, bareheaded

[centre]

QUICKSILVER

Accursed that ever I was saved or born!
How fatal is my sad arrival here!
As if the stars and Providence spake to me,   115
And said, 'The drift of all unlawful courses
(Whatever end they dare propose themselves
In frame of their licentious policies)
In the firm order of just Destiny,
They are the ready highways to our ruins'.   120
I know not what to do; my wicked hopes
Are, with this tempest, torn up by the roots!
O, which way shall I bend my desperate steps,
In which unsufferable shame and misery
Will not attend them? I will walk this bank   125
And see if I can meet the other relics
Of our poor, shipwrecked crew, or hear of them.
The knight—alas—was so far gone with wine,
And th'other three, that I refused their boat,
And took the hapless woman in another,   130
Who cannot but be sunk, whatever Fortune
Hath wrought upon the others' desperate lives.   *Exit*

Enter PETRONEL and SEAGULL, bareheaded

[downstage, right]

PETRONEL

Zounds, Captain! I tell thee, we are cast up o' the coast of
France! 'Sfoot, I am not drunk still, I hope! Dost remember
where we were last night?   135

---

106 *sort* crowd   112 *bareheaded* ed. (*bareheade* Q)   118 *frame* planning

---

106–7 *Wapping . . . gallows*. 'The usual place of execution for hanging of
   pirates and sea-rovers, at the low-water mark, and there to remain, till
   three tides had overflowed them'. John Stow, *The Survey of London*,
   ed. H. B. Wheatley (London, 1912; repr. 1965), p. 375. (Wapping
   gallows stood on a bend in the Thames, just below St Katherine's.)
131 *Fortune*. See note, IV, i, 1 s.d. *Cuckold's Haven*.

SEAGULL

No, by my troth, Knight, not I. But methinks we have been
a horrible while upon the water, and in the water.

PETRONEL

Ay me, we are undone for ever! Hast any money about thee?

SEAGULL

Not a penny, by heaven!

PETRONEL

Not a penny betwixt us, and cast ashore in France!   140

SEAGULL

Faith, I cannot tell that; my brains nor mine eyes are not
mine own yet.

Enter TWO GENTLEMEN

PETRONEL

'Sfoot, wilt not believe me? I know't by th'elevation of the
pole, and by the altitude and latitude of the climate. See,
here comes a couple of French gentlemen; I knew we were   145
in France; dost thou think our Englishmen are so Frenchified that a man knows not whether he be in France or in
England when he sees 'em? What shall we do? We must e'en
to 'em, and entreat some relief of 'em. Life is sweet, and we
have no other means to relieve our lives now, but their   150
charities.

SEAGULL

Pray you, do you beg on 'em then; you can speak French.

PETRONEL

*Monsieur, plaist-il d'avoir pitié de nostre grand infortunes. Je
suis un povre chevalier d'Angleterre qui a souffri l'infortune de
naufrage.*   155

1 GENTLEMAN

Un povre chevalier d'Angleterre?

PETRONEL

*Oui, monsieur, il est trop vraye; mais vous scavés bien nous
sommes toutes subject a fortune.*

2 GENTLEMAN

A poor knight of England? A poor knight of Windsor, are

154 *souffri l'infortune* (Qq *souffri'l infortune* Q)

---

143 *by th'elevation.* The latitude; another far-fetched pun.
146–7 *Frenchified.* cf. Fastidious Brisk in Jonson's *Every Man out of His
    Humour*, I, iii, 195; the aping of French manners was a common target
    of the Elizabethan satirist.
159 *A poor knight of Windsor.* A pensioner of the king who was allowed to live
    in the royal chambers at Windsor. By 1604 synonymous with 'pauper'.

you not? Why speak you this broken French when y'are a   160
whole Englishman? On what coast are you, think you?

PETRONEL

On the coast of France, sir.

1 GENTLEMAN

On the coast of Dogs, sir; y'are i'th' Isle o' Dogs, I tell you!
I see y'ave been washed in the Thames here, and I believe
ye were drowned in a tavern before, or else you would never   165
have took boat in such a dawning as this was. Farewell,
farewell; we will not know you for shaming of you.—I ken
the man weel; he's one of my thirty-pound knights.

2 GENTLEMAN

No, no, this is he that stole his knighthood o' the grand day
for four pound, giving to a page all the money in's purse, I   170
wot well.

Exeunt [GENTLEMEN]

SEAGULL

Death, Colonel! I knew you were overshot!

PETRONEL

Sure, I think now, indeed, Captain Seagull, we were something overshot.

Enter QUICKSILVER

What, my sweet Frank Quicksilver! Dost thou survive to   175
rejoice me? But what! Nobody at thy heels, Frank? Ay me,
what is become of poor Mistress Security?

QUICKSILVER

Faith, gone quite from her name, as she is from her fame,
I think; I left her to the mercy of the water.

SEAGULL

Let her go, let her go! Let us go to our ship at Blackwall, and   180
shift us.

---

172 *Death.* i.e., Christ's death   172 *overshot* wide of the mark; drunk

---

163 *Isle o' [of] Dogs.* A low swampy peninsula in the Thames opposite
Greenwich (see Appendix 1), well-known refuge for debtors and cut-
purses. Its proximity to the queen's castle makes it probable that the
play's title is a topical allusion to the royal sojourn there from mid-
March to mid-June 1605. It is also the place where Drake was knighted
and there may be further satirical play with the title of Jonson's
topical satire *Isle of Dogs*, for which he was imprisoned in 1597.

168 *thirty-pound knights.* Referring to James I's lavish creation of knights,
the subject of many a contemporary jest (cf. Appendix 1). This line was
evidently meant to mimic James's Scots accent.

PETRONEL

Nay, by my troth, let our clothes rot upon us, and let us rot
in them! Twenty to one our ship is attached by this time!
If we set her not under sail this last tide, I never looked for
any other. Woe, woe is me! What shall become of us? The   185
last money we could make, the greedy Thames has devoured,
and if our ship be attached, there is no hope can relieve us.

QUICKSILVER

'Sfoot, Knight, what an unknightly faintness transports thee!
Let our ship sink, and all the world that's without us be
taken from us, I hope I have some tricks in this brain of   190
mine shall not let us perish.

SEAGULL

Well said, Frank, i' faith. O my nimble-spirited Quicksilver!
'Fore God, would thou hadst been our colonel!

PETRONEL

I like his spirit rarely; but I see no means he has to support
that spirit.   195

QUICKSILVER

Go to, Knight! I have more means than thou art aware of.
I have not lived amongst goldsmiths and goldmakers all
this while, but I have learned something worthy of my time
with 'em. And not to let thee stink where thou stand'st,
Knight, I'll let thee know some of my skill presently.   200

SEAGULL

Do, good Frank, I beseech thee!

QUICKSILVER

I will blanch copper so cunningly that it shall endure all
proofs but the test: it shall endure malleation, it shall have
the ponderosity of Luna, and the tenacity of Luna, by no
means friable.   205

PETRONEL

'Slight, where learn'st thou these terms, trow?

QUICKSILVER

Tush, Knight, the terms of this art every ignorant quacksalver is perfect in. But I'll tell you how yourself shall blanch
copper thus cunningly. Take arsenic, otherwise called realgar

---

183 *attached* seized
203 *malleation* hammering
205 *friable* easily reduced to powder
208 *blanch* whiten, turn silvery

---

204 *ponderosity . . . tenacity of Luna.* The weight and toughness of silver.

(which, indeed, is plain ratsbane); sublime 'em three or four   210
times, then take the sublimate of this realgar, and put 'em
into a glass, into *chymia*, and let 'em have a convenient
decoction natural, four-and-twenty hours, and he will
become perfectly fixed; then take this fixed powder, and
project him upon well-purged copper, *et habebis magisterium*.   215
BOTH
Excellent Frank, let us hug thee!
QUICKSILVER
Nay, this I will do besides: I'll take you off twelvepence from
every angel, with a kind of *aqua fortis*, and never deface any
part of the image.
PETRONEL
But then it will want weight?   220
QUICKSILVER
You shall restore that thus: take your *sal achyme*, prepared,
and your distilled urine, and let your angels lie in it but four-
and-twenty hours, and they shall have their perfect weight
again. Come on, now, I hope this is enough to put some
spirit into the livers of you; I'll infuse more another time.   225
We have saluted the proud air long enough with our bare
sconces. Now will I have you to a wench's house of mine
at London; there make shift to shift us, and after, take such
fortunes as the stars shall assign us.
BOTH
Notable Frank, we will ever adore thee!   *Exeunt*   230

        Enter DRAWER, *with* WINIFRED, *new-attired*
                                                            [*stage left*]
WINIFRED
Now, sweet friend, you have brought me near enough your

210 *sublime* vaporize and solidify
211 *realgar* arsenic disulphide
212 *chymia* kemia, chemical analysis
216 s.p. BOTH ed. (*Ambo.* Q)
218 *aqua fortis* sulphuric acid
221 *sal achyme* salt without chyme
227 *sconces* skulls   230 s.p. BOTH ed. (*Ambo.* Q)

---

214 *fixed.* Made stable by being deprived of volatility or fluidity.
215 *et habebis magisterium.* Literally 'and you will have the philosopher's
    stone'. Ironical since Quicksilver will have only produced false silver.
226 *saluted the proud air* (Ayre Q). A possible pun on the name of the
    hero of Dekker's *The Shoemakers' Holiday*, Simon Eyre, who so closely
    resembles Touchstone.

tavern, which I desired that I might with some colour be
seen near, inquiring for my husband, who, I must tell you,
stole thither last night with my wet gown we have left at
your friend's—which, to continue your former honest kind-   235
ness, let me pray you to keep close from the knowledge of
any; and so, with all vow of your requital, let me now entreat
you to leave me to my woman's wit, and fortune.

DRAWER

All shall be done you desire; and so, all the fortune you can
wish for attend you!   *Exit* DRAWER   240

Enter SECURITY

SECURITY

I will once more to this unhappy tavern before I shift one
rag of me more, that I may there know what is left behind,
and what news of their passengers. I have bought me a hat
and band with the little money I had about me, and made
the streets a little leave staring at my night-cap.   245

WINIFRED

O my dear husband! Where have you been tonight? All
night abroad at taverns? Rob me of my garments, and fare
as one run away from me? Alas, is this seemly for a man of
your credit, of your age, and affection to your wife?

SECURITY

What should I say? How miraculously sorts this! Was not   250
I at home, and called thee last night?

WINIFRED

Yes, sir, the harmless sleep you broke, and my answer to
you, would have witnessed it, if you had had the patience
to have stayed and answered me: but your so sudden retreat
made me imagine you were gone to Master Bramble's, and   255
so rested patient and hopeful of your coming again, till this
your unbelieved absence brought me abroad with no less
than wonder, to seek you where the false knight had carried
you.

SECURITY

Villain and monster that I was, how have I abused thee! I   260
was suddenly gone indeed; for my sudden jealousy trans-
ferred me. I will say no more but this; dear wife, I suspected
thee.

WINIFRED

Did you suspect me?

SECURITY

Talk not of it, I beseech thee; I am ashamed to imagine it. 265

I will home, I will home; and every morning on my knees
ask thee heartily forgiveness.   *Exeunt*

SLITGUT

Now will I descend my honourable prospect, the farthest
seeing sea-mark of the world; no marvel, then, if I could
see two miles about me. I hope the red tempest's anger be   270
now overblown, which sure I think heaven sent as a punishment for profaning holy Saint Luke's memory with so
ridiculous a custom. Thou dishonest satyr, farewell to
honest married men; farewell to all sorts and degrees of
thee! Farewell, thou horn of hunger, that call'st th'Inns o'   275
Court to their manger! Farewell, thou horn of abundance,
that adornest the headsmen of the commonwealth! Farewell,
thou horn of direction, that is the city lanthorn! Farewell,
thou horn of pleasure, the ensign of the huntsman! Farewell, thou horn of destiny, th'ensign of the married man!   280
Farewell, thou horn tree, that bearest nothing but stone-
fruit!   *Exit*

268 s.p. SLITGUT ed. (unassigned Q)
275 *horn of hunger* dinner horn

---

270 *red tempest*. Red may indicate that alchemical change has taken place.
275–6 *Inns o' Court*. The London legal societies: Lincoln's Inn, Inner
  Temple, Middle Temple, and Gray's Inn.
275–82 *Farewell . . . stone-fruit*. The encomium on the horn is similar to
  Valerio's in Chapman, *All Fools* (1605).
276 *horn of abundance*. Cornucopia. Bulls' heads were set up by the Romans
  in honour of the river which brought wealth to the city, cf. Breton, op.
  cit., G1ᵛ.
277 *that adornest the headsmen*. Schelling notes the probable pun 'add-
  hornest', and 'headsmen' as cuckolds as well as dignitaries.
278 *horn of direction*. i.e., pun on lanthorn as 'land-horn', the transparent
  protective case made of 'horn' to shield a lantern from the wind.
281–2 *stone-fruit*. Stone = testicle, hence the tree is recognized as a phallic
  symbol.

Act IV, Scene ii

[A Room in TOUCHSTONE's *House]*

Enter TOUCHSTONE

TOUCHSTONE

Ha, sirrah! Thinks my Knight adventurer we can no point
of our compass? Do we not know north-north-east? north-
east-and-by-east? east-and-by-north? nor plain eastward?
Ha! Have we never heard of Virginia? Nor the Cavallaria?
Nor the Colonaria? Can we discover no discoveries? Well,   5
mine errant Sir Flash and my runagate Quicksilver, you
may drink drunk, crack cans, hurl away a brown dozen of
Monmouth caps or so, in sea ceremony to your *bon voyage*;
but for reaching any coast save the coast of Kent or Essex,
with this tide, or with this fleet, I'll be your warrant for a   10
Gravesend toast. There's that gone afore will stay your
admiral and vice-admiral and rear-admiral, were they all (as
they are) but one pinnace and under sail, as well as a remora,
doubt it not, and from this sconce, without either powder or
shot. 'Work upon that now'! Nay, and you'll show tricks,   15
we'll vie with you a little. My daughter, his lady, was sent
eastward by land to a castle of his i' the air (in what region
I know not) and, as I hear, was glad to take up her lodging
in her coach, she and her two waiting-women (her maid and
her mother), like three snails in a shell, and the coachman   20
a-top on 'em, I think. Since they have all found the way

---

1 *can* know
5 *Nor* Ed. (not Q)
15 *show tricks* pretend, make a fraud

4–5 *Cavallaria . . . Colonaria.* Latin law terms indicating the length of
   tenure for a knight and for an ordinary adventurer. Mocking Petronel's
   Virginian plans.
8 *Monmouth caps.* Flat caps worn by sailors and soldiers.
10 *I'll be your warrant.* I'll be bound. I wouldn't bet more than a Gravesend
   toast.
11 *Gravesend toast.* A phrase of uncertain meaning but denoting something
   worthless.
13 *pinnace.* Small two-masted schooner.
13 *remora.* A sucking fish. Traditionally believed to stay ships by attaching
   itself to the hull.
14 *sconce.* Crown of the head, with play on the sense 'fort'.

back again by Weeping Cross; but I'll not see 'em. And for
two on 'em, madam and her malkin, they are like to bite o'
the bridle for William, as the poor horses have done all this
while that hurried 'em, or else go graze o' the common.   25
So should my Dame Touchstone, too; but she has been my
cross these thirty years, and I'll now keep her, to fright away
sprites, i' faith. I wonder I hear no news of my son Golding.
He was sent for to the Guildhall this morning betimes, and
I marvel at the matter. If I had not laid up comfort and hope   30
in him, I should grow desperate of all.

Enter GOLDING

See, he is come i' my thought! How now, son? What news
at the Court of Aldermen?
GOLDING
Troth, sir, an accident somewhat strange, else it hath little
in it worth the reporting.   35
TOUCHSTONE
What? It is not borrowing of money, then?
GOLDING
No, sir; it hath pleased the worshipful commoners of the
City to take me one i' their number at presentation of the
inquest—
TOUCHSTONE
Ha!   40
GOLDING
And the alderman of the ward wherein I dwell to appoint
me his deputy—
TOUCHSTONE
How!
GOLDING
In which place I have had an oath ministered me, since I
went.   45

23 *malkin* slut
32 *i'my* ... just as I ... 32 s.d. ed. (34 s.d. Q)

22 *Weeping Cross.* Eleanor cross (erected by Edward I in memory of his
    first queen, Eleanor of Castile (d. 1290)), of which there were six in
    England. To return by the Weeping Cross was to return repentant.
    Proverbial. Tilley, W248.
23–4 *bite o' the bridle for William.* Proverbial. Tilley, B670; to fare badly,
    to be cut short, to suffer want.
38–9 *presentation of the inquest.* Report to a committee of inquiry.

TOUCHSTONE
> Now, my dear and happy son! Let me kiss thy new worship,
> and a little boast mine own happiness in thee. What a fortune
> was it (or rather my judgement, indeed) for me, first to see
> that in his disposition which a whole city so conspires to
> second! Ta'en into the livery of his company the first day   50
> of his freedom! Now (not a week married) chosen com-
> moner and alderman's deputy in a day! Note but the reward
> of a thrifty course. The wonder of his time! Well, I will
> honour Master Alderman for this act (as becomes me) [*doffing
> his cap*] and shall think the better of the Common Council's   55
> wisdom and worship while I live, for thus meeting, or but
> coming after me, in the opinion of his desert. Forward, my
> sufficient son, and as this is the first, so esteem it the least step
> to that high and prime honour that expects thee.

GOLDING
> Sir, as I was not ambitious of this, so I covet no higher   60
> place; it hath dignity enough, if it will but save me from
> contempt; and I had rather my bearing in this or any other
> office should add worth to it, than the place give the least
> opinion to me.

TOUCHSTONE
> Excellently spoken! This modest answer of thine blushes, as   65
> if it said, I will wear scarlet shortly. Worshipful son! I
> cannot contain myself, I must tell thee: I hope to see thee one
> o' the monuments of our City, and reckoned among her
> worthies, to be remembered the same day with the Lady
> Ramsey and grave Gresham, when the famous fable of   70

46 *me* Q3 (we Q)
51–2 *commoner* member of the Common Council
56 *worship* repute, good name
58 *sufficient* capable
59 *expects* awaits
64 *opinion* good reputation
66 *wear scarlet* be an alderman and wear red velvet

50 *Ta'en . . . livery.* On the same day that Touchstone has declared his
   apprenticeship complete (making him a freeman able to set up his own
   business), the select 'livery men' of the Goldsmiths' company have
   remarkably elevated him to their rank.
69–70 *Lady Ramsey.* Widow of the Lord Mayor, who, in 1577, founded
   Christ's Hospital.
70 *Gresham.* Sir Thomas Gresham, founder of the Royal Exchange.

5

Whittington and his puss shall be forgotten, and thou and
thy acts become the posies for hospitals; when thy name
shall be written upon conduits, and thy deeds played i' thy
lifetime by the best companies of actors, and be called their
get-penny. This I divine; this I prophesy.   75

GOLDING

Sir, engage not your expectation farther than my abilities
will answer. I, that know mine own strengths, fear 'em; and
there is so seldom a loss in promising the least, that commonly it brings with it a welcome deceit. I have other news
for you, sir.   80

TOUCHSTONE

None more welcome, I am sure!

GOLDING

They have their degree of welcome, I dare affirm. The
colonel, and all his company, this morning putting forth
drunk from Billingsgate, had like to have been cast away o'
this side Greenwich; and (as I have intelligence, by a false   85
brother) are come dropping to town like so many masterless
men, i' their doublets and hose, without hat, or cloak, or any
other—

TOUCHSTONE

A miracle! The justice of heaven! Where are they? Let's go
presently and lay for 'em.   90

GOLDING

I have done that already, sir, both by constables, and other
officers, who shall take 'em at their old Anchor, and with less
tumult or suspicion than if yourself were seen in't, under

---

75 *get-penny* box-office success
85–6 *false brother* traitor, informer
90 *lay for 'em* set an ambush or trap

---

71 *Whittington and his puss.* Sir Richard Whittington was a mercer and
three times Lord Mayor of London, remembered for the endowments
he left behind after his death in 1423. The legend of the cat, which has
close similarities with German folk tales, first appeared in English in a
(lost) play performed by the Prince's Servants, 8 February 1605
(Stationers' Register).

72 *posies.* Motto inscribed to the wealthy citizens who donated funds to
build conduits and hospitals.

73–4 *deeds played i' thy lifetime.* This happened to Gresham in a Latin play
by I. Rickets, 1570. Citizen heroes were popular figures, e.g., Heywood's
If You Know Not Me, You Know Nobody, Part II (1605), in which
Whittington, Lady Ramsey, and Gresham are portrayed.

colour of a great press that is now abroad, and they shall
here be brought afore me.   95

TOUCHSTONE
Prudent and politic son! Disgrace 'em all that ever thou
canst; their ship I have already arrested. How to my wish
it falls out, that thou hast the place of a justicer upon 'em!
I am partly glad of the injury done to me, that thou may'st
punish it. Be severe i' thy place, like a new officer o' the first   100
quarter, unreflected. You hear how our lady is come back
with her train from the invisible castle?

GOLDING
No; where is she?

TOUCHSTONE
Within; but I ha' not seen her yet, nor her mother, who now
begins to wish her daughter undubbed, they say, and that   105
she had walked a foot-pace with her sister. Here they come;
stand back.

        [*Enter*] MISTRESS TOUCHSTONE, GERTRUDE, MILDRED,
                            SINDEFY

God save your Ladyship, 'save your good Ladyship! Your
Ladyship is welcome from your enchanted castle, so are
your beauteous retinue. I hear your knight-errant is travelled   110
on strange adventures. Surely, in my mind, your Ladyship
'hath fished fair and caught a frog', as the saying is.

MISTRESS TOUCHSTONE
Speak to your father, Madam, and kneel down.

GERTRUDE
Kneel? I hope I am not brought so low yet! Though my
knight be run away, and has sold my land, I am a lady still!   115

TOUCHSTONE
Your Ladyship says true, Madam; and it is fitter, and a
greater decorum, that I should curtsey to you that are a
knight's wife, and a lady, than you be brought o' your knees
to me, who am a poor cullion, and your father.

108 s.d. [*Enter*] MISTRESS TOUCHSTONE, etc. (*Touchstone* and *Goulding*
        included in Q)
112 *fished fair and caught a frog* proverbial. Tilley, F767
119 *cullion* base, despicable, vile fellow

93–4 *under colour . . . press.* Under the pretext of drafting troops or sailors.
101 *unreflected.* A pun: as an officer of the first term, not to be deflected
     from his duty; and as the crescent moon, not reflecting much light.
106 *a foot-pace.* To forego the 'court-amble' for a staid pace.

GERTRUDE

Law! My father knows his duty.   120

MISTRESS TOUCHSTONE

O child!

TOUCHSTONE

And therefore I do desire your Ladyship, my good Lady
Flash, in all humility, to depart my obscure cottage, and
return in quest of your bright and most transparent castle,
'however presently concealed to mortal eyes'. And as for one   125
poor woman of your train here, I will take that order, she
shall no longer be a charge unto you, nor help to spend your
Ladyship; she shall stay at home with me, and not go abroad;
not put you to the pawning of an odd coach-horse or three
wheels, but take part with the Touchstone. If we lack, we   130
will not complain to your Ladyship. And so, good Madam,
with your damsel here, please you to let us see your straight
backs, in equipage; for truly, here is no roost for such
chickens as you are, or birds o' your feather, if it like your
Ladyship.   135

GERTRUDE

Marry, fist o' your kindness! I thought as much. Come
away, Sin. We shall as soon get a fart from a dead man, as a
farthing of courtesy here.

MILDRED

O good sister!

GERTRUDE

Sister, sir-reverence? Come away, I say, hunger drops out   140
at his nose.

GOLDING

O Madam, 'fair words never hurt the tongue'.

GERTRUDE

How say you by that? You   out with your gold-ends
now!

MISTRESS TOUCHSTONE

Stay, Lady-daughter! Good husband!   145

133 *in equipage* at quick march
136 *fist* corruption of foist, i.e., fart
137–8 *get a fart . . . here* proverbial. Tilley, F63
140–1 *hunger . . . nose* proverbial. Tilley, H813
142 *fair words . . . tongue* proverbial. Tilley, W793
143 *gold-ends* moral tags

124 *transparent castle.* Easily seen through. cf. 'build castles in the air',
proverbial. Tilley, C126.

TOUCHSTONE

Wife, no man loves his fetters, be they made of gold. I list
not ha' my head fastened under my child's girdle; as she has
brewed, so let her drink, o' God's name! She went witless
to wedding, now she may go wisely a-begging. It's but
honeymoon yet with her ladyship; she has coach-horses,   150
apparel, jewels, yet left; she needs care for no friends, nor
take knowledge of father, mother, brother, sister, or anybody. When those are pawned or spent, perhaps we shall
return into the list of her acquaintance.

GERTRUDE

I scorn it, i'faith! Come, Sin!   155

MISTRESS TOUCHSTONE

O Madam, why do you provoke your father thus?

                              Exit GERTRUDE [*with* SINDEFY]

TOUCHSTONE

Nay, nay; e'en let pride go afore, shame will follow after,
I warrant you. Come, why dost thou weep now? Thou art
not the first good cow hast had an ill calf, I trust.

                              [*Exit* MISTRESS TOUCHSTONE *and*]

                    Enter CONSTABLE

What's the news with that fellow?   160

GOLDING

Sir, the knight and your man Quicksilver are without; will
you ha' 'em brought in?

TOUCHSTONE

O, by any means!

                              [*Exit* CONSTABLE]

And, son, here's a chair; appear terrible unto 'em on the
first interview. Let them behold the melancholy of a   165
magistrate, and taste the fury of a citizen in office.

---

146 *no man . . . gold* proverbial. Tilley, M338
147 *head fastened . . . girdle* proverbial. Tilley, H248
147–8 *as she has brewed*, etc. proverbial. Tilley, B654
157 s.d. ed. (156 s.d. Q)
157 *e'en let pride . . . after* proverbial. Tilley, P576
159 *good cow . . . calf* proverbial. Tilley, C761
160 s.d. *Enter* CONSTABLE ed. (159 s.d. *Enter Const.* Q)
165 *melancholy* (rare sense) irascibility

148–9 *She went . . . a-begging.* Heywood's *Proverbs*, I, chapter 11.

GOLDING

Why, sir, I can do nothing to 'em, except you charge 'em
with somewhat.

TOUCHSTONE

I will charge 'em and recharge 'em, rather than authority
should want foil to set it off.   170

[*Offers* GOLDING *a chair*]

GOLDING

No, good sir, I will not.

TOUCHSTONE

Son, it is your place, by any means!

GOLDING

Believe it, I will not, sir.

Enter KNIGHT PETRONEL, QUICKSILVER, CONSTABLE,
OFFICERS

PETRONEL

How misfortune pursues us still in our misery!

QUICKSILVER

Would it had been my fortune to have been trussed up at   175
Wapping, rather than ever ha' come here!

PETRONEL

Or mine to have famished in the island!

QUICKSILVER

Must Golding sit upon us?

CONSTABLE

You might carry an M. under your girdle to Master Deputy's
worship.   180

GOLDING

What are those, Master Constable?

CONSTABLE

An't please your worship, a couple of masterless men I
pressed for the Low Countries, sir.

170 *foil*. A piece of gold placed under a gem to enhance its lustre.
175 *trussed up*. Hanged on the gallows. See above, note IV, i, 106–7.
177 *in the island*. i.e., the Isle of Dogs. See above, note IV, i, 163.
179 *carry an M. under your girdle*. M. = abbrev. for master, i.e., to use
    respectful language when addressing one's superiors. Tilley, M1.

GOLDING
Why do you not carry 'em to Bridewell, according to your
order, they may be shipped away?   185
CONSTABLE
An't please your worship, one of 'em says he is a knight;
and we thought good to show him to your worship, for our
discharge.
GOLDING
Which is he?
CONSTABLE
This, sir!   190
GOLDING
And what's the other?
CONSTABLE
A knight's fellow, sir, an't please you.
GOLDING
What! A knight and his fellow thus accoutred? Where are
their hats and feathers, their rapiers and their cloaks?
QUICKSILVER
O, they mock us!   195
CONSTABLE
Nay, truly, sir, they had cast both their feathers and hats
too, before we see 'em. Here's all their furniture, an't please
you, that we found. They say knights are now to be known
without feathers, like cockerels by their spurs, sir.
GOLDING
What are their names, say they?   200
TOUCHSTONE
[Aside] Very well, this! He should not take knowledge of
'em in his place, indeed.
CONSTABLE
This is Sir Petronel Flash.
TOUCHSTONE
How!

187–8 *for our discharge* claiming a fee

---

184 *Bridewell*. House of correction since 1553. Originally founded as a
    monastery, near St Bride's Church, Fleet Street. Petronel and Quick-
    silver were to be held there under the Statute against vagabonds and
    masterless men (1597), until being conscripted into the army serving
    in the Low Countries. (See Stow, *The Survey of London*, ed. Wheatley,
    p. 440.)
194 *feathers*. The most conspicuous mark of foppery.

CONSTABLE

And this, Francis Quicksilver.   205

TOUCHSTONE

Is't possible? I thought your worship had been gone for
Virginia, sir. You are welcome home, sir. Your worship has
made a quick return, it seems, and no doubt a good voyage.
Nay, pray you be covered, sir. How did your biscuit hold
out, sir? Methought I had seen this gentleman afore. Good   210
Master Quicksilver, how a degree to the southward has
changed you!

GOLDING

Do you know 'em, father?—forbear your offers a little, you
shall be heard anon.

TOUCHSTONE

Yes, Master Deputy; I had a small venture with them in   215
the voyage—a thing called a son-in-law, or so. Officers, you
may let 'em stand alone, they will not run away; I'll give my
word for them. A couple of very honest gentlemen! One of
'em was my prentice, Master Quicksilver here; and when he
had two year to serve, kept his whore and his hunting nag,   220
would play his hundred pound at gresco, or primero, as
familiarly (and all o' my purse) as any bright piece of
crimson on 'em all; had his changeable trunks of apparel
standing at livery, with his mare, his chest of perfumed
linen, and his bathing-tubs: which when I told him of, why   225
he—he was a gentleman, and I a poor Cheapside groom!
The remedy was, we must part. Since when, he hath had
the gift of gathering up some small parcels of mine, to the
value of five hundred pound, dispersed among my customers,
to furnish this his Virginian venture; wherein this knight was   230
the chief, Sir Flash—one that married a daughter of mine,
ladyfied her, turned two thousand pounds' worth of good
land of hers into cash within the first week, bought her a
new gown and a coach, sent her to seek her fortune by land,

---

221 *gresco, or primero* card games

---

209 *be covered.* Put on your hat, a sarcastic hit at Petronel's having lost
his hat.

209 *biscuit.* Store of ship's biscuits, the staple ration of seamen.

211 *degree to the southward.* Probably mocking Quicksilver's frequenting of
the public theatres in Southwark.

213 *offers.* [*to* CONSTABLE] evidence, or [*to* PRISONERS] petitions.

222-3 *bright piece of crimson.* Scarlet was the colour worn by nobles and
court officials. It is also the colour of 'infected' mercury.

whilst himself prepared for his fortune by sea; took in fresh   235
flesh at Billingsgate, for his own diet, to serve him the whole
voyage—the wife of a certain usurer, called Security, who
hath been the broker for 'em in all this business. Please,
Master Deputy, 'work upon that now'!

GOLDING

If my worshipful father have ended.   240

TOUCHSTONE

I have, it shall please Master Deputy.

GOLDING

Well then, under correction—

TOUCHSTONE

Now, son, come over 'em with some fine gird, as, thus:
'Knight, you shall be encountered', that is, had to the
Counter, or, 'Quicksilver, I will put you in a crucible', or   245
so—

GOLDING

Sir Petronel Flash, I am sorry to see such flashes as these
proceed from a gentleman of your quality and rank; for mine
own part, I could wish I could say I could not see them;
but such is the misery of magistrates and men in place, that   250
they must not wink at offenders. Take him aside: I will hear
you anon, sir.

TOUCHSTONE

I like this well, yet; there's some grace i' the knight left—
he cries!

GOLDING

Francis Quicksilver, would God thou hadst turned quack-   255
salver, rather than run into these dissolute and lewd courses!
It is great pity; thou art a proper young man, of an honest
and clean face, somewhat near a good one (God hath done
his part in thee); but thou hast made too much and been
too proud of that face, with the rest of thy body; for main-   260
tenance of which in neat and garish attire (only to be looked

242 *under correction* confinement and corporal punishment
243 *gird* sharp stroke, blow
255-6 *quacksalver* charlatan, quack

244-5 *encountered . . . the Counter.* This pun is used in *Westward Ho!*, ed.
   Bowers, III, ii, 76. 'I will patiently incounter the Counter'.
245 *Quicksilver, I will put you in a crucible.* Touchstone believes that
   imprisonment and his own wrath will purge the tainted mercury.
250 *men in place.* Ministers of state in the service of the Crown.

upon by some light housewives) thou hast prodigally con-
sumed much of thy master's estate; and being by him gently
admonished, at several times, hast returned thyself haughty
and rebellious in thine answers, thundering out uncivil   265
comparisons, requiting all his kindness with a coarse and
harsh behaviour, never returning thanks for any one benefit,
but receiving all, as if they had been debts to thee and no
courtesies. I must tell thee, Francis, these are manifest signs
of an ill nature; and God doth often punish such pride   270
and *outrecuidance* with scorn and infamy, which is the worst
of misfortune. My worshipful father, what do you please
to charge them withal? From the press I will free 'em,
Master Constable.

CONSTABLE
Then I'll leave your worship, sir.   275

GOLDING
No, you may stay; there will be other matters against 'em.

TOUCHSTONE
Sir, I do charge this gallant, Master Quicksilver, on suspicion of felony; and the knight as being accessory in the
receipt of my goods.

QUICKSILVER
O God, sir!   280

TOUCHSTONE
Hold thy peace, impudent varlet, hold thy peace! With
what forehead or face dost thou offer to chop logic with me,
having run such a race of riot as thou hast done? Does not
the sight of this worshipful man's fortune and temper con-
found thee, that was thy younger fellow in household, and   285
now come to have the place of a judge upon thee? Dost not
observe this? Which of all thy gallants and gamesters, thy
swearers and thy swaggerers, will come now to moan thy
misfortune, or pity thy penury? They'll look out at a window,
as thou rid'st in triumph to Tyburn, and cry, 'Yonder goes   290
honest Frank, mad Quicksilver'! 'He was a free boon com-
panion, when he had money', says one; 'Hang him, fool'!
says another, 'he could not keep it when he had it'! 'A pox
o' the cullion, his master', says a third, 'he has brought him
to this'; when their pox of pleasure, and their piles of perdi-   295
tion, would have been better bestowed upon thee, that hast

271 *outrecuidance* arrogance, overbearing conceit
282 *chop logic* bicker, exchange disrespectful argument
295–6 *pox of pleasure . . . piles of perdition* infectious malice and
    pointed detraction

ventured for 'em with the best, and by the clew of thy
knavery, brought thyself weeping to the cart of calamity.

QUICKSILVER

Worshipful master!

TOUCHSTONE

Offer not to speak, crocodile; I will not hear a sound come   300
from thee. Thou hast learnt to whine at the play yonder.
Master Deputy, pray you commit 'em both to safe custody,
till I be able farther to charge 'em.

QUICKSILVER

O me, what an infortunate thing am I!

PETRONEL

Will you not take security, sir?   305

TOUCHSTONE

Yes, marry, will I, Sir Flash, if I can find him, and charge
him as deep as the best on you. He has been the plotter of
all this; he is your engineer, I hear. Master Deputy, you'll
dispose of these? In the meantime, I'll to my Lord Mayor,
and get his warrant to seize that serpent Security into my   310
hands, and seal up both house and goods to the King's use
or my satisfaction.

GOLDING

Officers, take 'em to the Counter.

QUICKSILVER ⎱
PETRONEL   ⎰

O God!

TOUCHSTONE

Nay, on, on! You see the issue of your sloth. Of sloth cometh   315
pleasure, of pleasure cometh riot, of riot comes whoring,
of whoring comes spending, of spending comes want, of
want comes theft, of theft comes hanging; and there is my
Quicksilver fixed.   *Exeunt*

305 *take security* accept bail
308 *engineer* schemer

297 *clew*. Ball of thread; fig. that which guides through intricate courses.
298 *cart of calamity*. The cart which bears criminals to Tyburn.
306 *if I can find him*. Picks up the pun in 305.
310 *serpent*. Security once more associated with the Morality Play Vice.
319 *fixed*. Another example of Touchstone's naïve belief in alchemical cure.

Act V, Scene i

[GERTRUDE's *Lodging*]

GERTRUDE, SINDEFY

GERTRUDE

Ah, Sin! hast thou ever read i'the chronicle of any lady and
her waiting-woman driven to that extremity that we are,
Sin?

SINDEFY

Not I, truly, Madam; and if I had, it were but cold comfort
should come out of books now.   5

GERTRUDE

Why, good faith, Sin, I could dine with a lamentable story
now. *O hone, hone, o no nera*, &c. Canst thou tell ne'er a
one, Sin?

SINDEFY

None but mine own, Madam, which is lamentable enough:
first to be stolen from my friends, which were worshipful   10
and of good accompt, by a prentice in the habit and disguise
of a gentleman, and here brought up to London and promised marriage, and now likely to be forsaken, for he is in
possibility to be hanged!

GERTRUDE

Nay, weep not, good Sin; my Petronel is in as good possi-   15
bility as he. Thy miseries are nothing to mine, Sin; I was
more than promised marriage, Sin; I had it, Sin, and was
made a lady; and by a knight, Sin; which is now as good as
no knight, Sin. And I was born in London, which is more
than brought up, Sin; and already forsaken, which is past   20
likelihood, Sin; and instead of land i' the country, all my
knight's living lies i' the Counter, Sin; there's his castle now!

SINDEFY

Which he cannot be forced out of, Madam.

GERTRUDE

Yes, if he would live hungry a week or two. 'Hunger', they
say, 'breaks stone walls'! But he is e'en well enough served,   25
Sin, that so soon as ever he had got my hand to the sale of
my inheritance, run away from me, and I had been his punk,

4 *cold comfort* proverbial. Tilley, C542
24–5 *Hunger . . . stone walls* proverbial. Tilley, H811

7 '*O hone, hone, o no nera*'. Refrain from an Irish lament.

God bless us! Would the Knight o' the Sun, or Palmerin of
England, have used their ladies so, Sin? or Sir Lancelot? or
Sir Tristram?   30

SINDEFY

I do not know, Madam.

GERTRUDE

Then thou know'st nothing, Sin. Thou art a fool, Sin. The
knighthood nowadays are nothing like the knighthood of old
time. They rid a-horseback; ours go a-foot. They were
attended by their squires; ours by their lackeys. They went   35
buckled in their armour; ours muffled in their cloaks. They
travelled wildernesses and deserts; ours dare scarce walk the
streets. They were still pressed to engage their honour; ours
still ready to pawn their clothes. They would gallop on at
sight of a monster; ours run away at sight of a sergeant.   40
They would help poor ladies; ours make poor ladies.

SINDEFY

Ay, Madam, they were Knights of the Round Table at
Winchester, that sought adventures; but these of the Square
Table at ordinaries, that sit at hazard—

GERTRUDE

True, Sin, let him vanish. And tell me, what shall we pawn   45
next?

SINDEFY

Ay, marry, Madam, a timely consideration; for our hostess
(profane woman!) has sworn by bread and salt, she will not
trust us another meal.

---

44 *hazard* a game of dice

---

28 *Knight o' [of] the Sun.* Hero of the first part of *The Mirror of Princely
   Deeds and Knighthood* by Diego Ortuñez, first translated into English
   by Margaret Tyler in 1578.

28–9 *Palmerin of England.* By Luis Hurtado, translated into English by
   Anthony Munday in 1596. Such Spanish romances were extremely
   popular with the London citizenry. cf. *The Knight of the Burning Pestle*,
   I, iii, s.d.: '*Enter* RAFE *like a Grocer in's shop, with Two Prentices Reading
   Palmerin of England*'.

33–41 *knighthood . . . ladies.* A popular complaint of the time. See
   Appendix 1.

40 *sergeant.* Sheriff's officer whose duty it was to arrest debtors.

43 *Winchester.* Thought in the seventeenth century to be the seat of
   King Arthur's Court, and where his supposed table, with the figure of
   the king painted in the middle, still remains.

GERTRUDE

Let it stink in her hand then! I'll not be beholding to her.   50
Let me see: my jewels be gone, and my gowns, and my red
velvet petticoat that I was married in, and my wedding silk
stockings, and all thy best apparel, poor Sin! Good faith,
rather than thou shouldst pawn a rag more, I'd lay my Ladyship in lavender—if I knew where.   55

SINDEFY

Alas, Madam, your Ladyship?

GERTRUDE

Ay, why? You do not scorn my Ladyship, though it is in a
waistcoat? God's my life, you are a peat indeed! Do I offer to
mortgage my Ladyship, for you and for your avail, and do
you turn the lip and the alas to my Ladyship?   60

SINDEFY

No, Madam; but I make question who will lend anything
upon it?

GERTRUDE

Who? Marry, enow, I warrant you, if you'll seek 'em out.
I'm sure I remember the time when I would ha' given a
thousand pound (if I had had it) to have been a lady; and   65
I hope I was not bred and born with that appetite alone:
some other gentleborn o' the City have the same longing, I
trust. And for my part, I would afford 'em a penny'rth; my
Ladyship is little the worse for the wearing, and yet I would
bate a good deal of the sum. I would lend it (let me see) for   70
forty pound in hand, Sin—that would apparel us—and ten
pound a year. That would keep me and you, Sin (with our
needles)—and we should never need to be beholding to our
scurvy parents! Good Lord, that there are no fairies nowadays, Sin!   75

SINDEFY

Why, Madam?

50 *beholding* obliged
54–5 *lay . . . in lavender* pawn. Proverbial. Tilley, L96
57–8 *in a waistcoat* in shirt-sleeves
58 *peat* term of endearment for a girl or woman
60 *turn the lip* show contempt
63 *enow* enough
68 *penny'rth* pennyworth, i.e., money's worth
69 *worse for the wearing* proverbial. Tilley, W207
70 *bate* bring down the price
72–3 *with our needles* with what we can earn by needlework

GERTRUDE

To do miracles, and bring ladies money. Sure, if we lay in a
cleanly house, they would haunt it, Sin? I'll try. I'll sweep
the chamber soon at night, and set a dish of water o' the
hearth. A fairy may come, and bring a pearl or a diamond.   80
We do not know, Sin? Or, there may be a pot of gold hid o'
the backside, if we had tools to dig for't? Why may not we
two rise early i' the morning, Sin, afore anybody is up, and
find a jewel i' the streets worth a hundred pound? May not
some great court-lady, as she comes from revels at midnight,   85
look out of her coach as 'tis running, and lose such a jewel,
and we find it? Ha?

SINDEFY

They are pretty waking dreams, these.

GERTRUDE

Or may not some old usurer be drunk overnight, with a
bag of money, and leave it behind him on a stall? For God-   90
sake, Sin, let's rise tomorrow by break of day, and see! I
protest, law! if I had as much money as an alderman, I
would scatter some of it i' the streets for poor ladies to find,
when their knights were laid up. And now I remember my
song o' the Golden Shower, why may not I have such a   95
fortune? I'll sing it, and try what luck I shall have after it.

[Sings]

Fond fables tell of old
How Jove in Danaë's lap
Fell in a shower of gold,
By which she caught a clap;   100
O had it been my hap

(How e'er the blow doth threaten)
So well I like the play,
That I could wish all day
And night to be so beaten.   105

Enter MISTRESS TOUCHSTONE

82 *backside* behind the house   93 *of it* ed. (on 't Q)

95–105 *song o' the Golden Shower.* From the Greek myth. Zeus appears in
a shower of gold to seduce Danaë in the cell where her father imprisoned
her. (cf. T. Bateson, Madrigal IX, *The English Madrigal School*, ed.
Fellowes, XXI, p. xi.)

100 *caught a clap.* i.e., made pregnant. Gertrude wishes to become pregnant
in this way so that she can have sexual intercourse with a god and also
have the gold in which he manifests himself.

O here's my mother! Good luck, I hope. Ha' you brought
any money, mother? Pray you, mother, your blessing. Nay,
sweet mother, do not weep.

MISTRESS TOUCHSTONE

God bless you! I would I were in my grave!

GERTRUDE

Nay, dear mother, can you steal no more money from my 110
father? Dry your eyes, and comfort me. Alas, it is my knight's
fault, and not mine, that I am in a waistcoat, and attired thus
simply.

MISTRESS TOUCHSTONE

Simply? 'Tis better than thou deserv'st. Never whimper for
the matter. 'Thou shouldst have looked before thou hadst 115
leaped'. Thou wert afire to be lady, and now your Ladyship
and you may both blow at the coal, for aught I know. 'Self do,
self have'. 'The hasty person never wants woe', they say.

GERTRUDE

Nay, then, mother, you should ha' looked to it. A body
would think you were the older; I did but my kind, I. He 120
was a knight, and I was fit to be a lady. 'Tis not lack of liking,
but lack of living, that severs us. And you talk like yourself
and a cittiner in this, i' faith. You show what husband you
come on, I wis: you smell o'the Touchstone—he that will
do more for his daughter that he has married [to] a scurvy 125
gold-end man, and his prentice, than he will for his tother
daughter, that has wedded a knight, and his customer. By
this light, I think he is not my legitimate father.

SINDEFY

O good Madam, do not take up your mother so!

MISTRESS TOUCHSTONE

Nay, nay, let her e'en alone! Let her Ladyship grieve me 130
still, with her bitter taunts and terms. I have not dole enough
to see her in this miserable case, I, without her velvet gowns,

115–16 *shouldst have looked . . . leaped* proverbial. Tilley, L429
117 *blow at the coal* proverbial. Tilley, C460
117–18 *Self do, self have* proverbial. Tilley, S217
118 *hasty . . . woe* proverbial. Tilley, M159
120 *my kind* according to my nature and right of birth
123 *cittiner* colloquial for citizen
124 I *wis* forsooth
124 *o' the* Ed. (the Q)
125 *to* Ed. (omitted in Q)

124 *come on.* Pun: come from, and probable sexual connotation.

without ribands, without jewels, without French wires, or
cheat-bread, or quails, or a little dog, or a gentleman-usher,
or anything, indeed, that's fit for a lady—   135

SINDEFY
[*Aside*] Except her tongue.

MISTRESS TOUCHSTONE
And I not able to relieve her, neither, being kept so short
by my husband. Well, God knows my heart. I did little
think that ever she should have had need of her sister
Golding.   140

GERTRUDE
Why, mother, I ha' not yet. Alas, good mother, be not
intoxicate for me; I am well enough. I would not change
husbands with my sister, I. 'The leg of a lark is better than
the body of a kite'.

MISTRESS TOUCHSTONE
I know that, but—   145

GERTRUDE
What, sweet mother, what?

MISTRESS TOUCHSTONE
It's but ill food when nothing's left but the claw.

GERTRUDE
That's true, mother. Ay me!

MISTRESS TOUCHSTONE
Nay, sweet lady-bird, sigh not! Child, Madam, why do you
weep thus? Be of good cheer; I shall die, if you cry and mar   150
your complexion thus.

GERTRUDE
Alas, mother, what should I do?

MISTRESS TOUCHSTONE
Go to thy sister's, child; she'll be proud thy Ladyship will
come under her roof. She'll win thy father to release thy
knight, and redeem thy gowns and thy coach and thy horses,   155
and set thee up again.

GERTRUDE
But will she get him to set my knight up too?

MISTRESS TOUCHSTONE
That she will, or anything else thou'lt ask her.

133 *French wires* supports for the hair and ruff
134 *cheat-bread* inferior bread
142 *intoxicate* intemperate, exasperated
143–4 *leg of a lark . . . kite* proverbial. Tilley, L186

GERTRUDE
I will begin to love her, if I thought she would do this.

MISTRESS TOUCHSTONE
Try her, good chuck, I warrant thee.   160

GERTRUDE
Dost thou think she'll do't?

SINDEFY
Ay, Madam, and be glad you will receive it.

MISTRESS TOUCHSTONE
That's a good maiden; she tells you true. Come, I'll take
order for your debts i' the ale-house.

GERTRUDE
Go, Sin, and pray for thy Frank, as I will for my Pet.   165

[*Exeunt*]

[Act V, Scene ii

Goldsmith's Row]

Enter TOUCHSTONE, GOLDING, WOLF

TOUCHSTONE
I will receive no letters, Master Wolf; you shall pardon me.

GOLDING
Good father, let me entreat you.

TOUCHSTONE
Son Golding, I will not be tempted; I find mine own easy
nature, and I know not what a well-penned subtle letter may
work upon it; there may be tricks, packing, do you see?   5
Return with your packet, sir.

WOLF
Believe it, sir, you need fear no packing here; these are but
letters of submission, all.

TOUCHSTONE
Sir, I do look for no submission. I will bear myself in this
like blind Justice. 'Work upon that now'! When the Sessions   10
come, they shall hear from me.

GOLDING
From whom come your letters, Master Wolf?

WOLF
An't please you, sir, one from Sir Petronel, another from

160 *chuck* term of endearment
  3 *find* perceive
  5 *packing* scheming

Francis Quicksilver, and a third from old Security, who is
almost mad in prison. There are two to your worship; one   15
from Master Francis, sir, another from the knight.

TOUCHSTONE

I do wonder, Master Wolf, why you should travail thus in a
business so contrary to kind or the nature o' your place!
That you, being the keeper of a prison, should labour the
release of your prisoners! Whereas, methinks, it were far   20
more natural and kindly in you to be ranging about for more,
and not let these 'scape you have already under the tooth.
But they say, you wolves, when you ha' sucked the blood
once, that they are dry, you ha' done.

WOLF

Sir, your worship may descant as you please o' my name;   25
but I protest I was never so mortified with any men's discourse or behaviour in prison; yet I have had of all sorts of
men i' the kingdom under my keys, and almost of all
religions i' the land, as: Papist, Protestant, Puritan, Brownist, Anabaptist, Millenary, Family-o'-Love, Jew, Turk,   30
Infidel, Atheist, Good Fellow, &c.

GOLDING

And which of all these, thinks Master Wolf, was the best
religion?

WOLF

Troth, Master Deputy, they that pay fees best: we never
examine their consciences farder.   35

---

25 *descant* comment, remark
26 *mortified* (rare sense) overcome, depressed
28 *under my keys* under lock and key
31 *Good Fellow* reveller

19–20 *That you ... prisoners.* The gaoler accepted fees from prisoners for
   food, lodging, and other favours.
21 *kindly.* Pun: showing favour, and according to your profession.
22 *tooth.* Fig. gaol; play on name Wolf.
29–30 *Brownist.* i.e., follower of Robert Brown (1550–1633); one of the
   strictest evangelical Protestant sects.
30 *Millenary.* Believing in the Second Coming of Christ, when He would
   reign for a thousand years until the Day of Judgement.
30 *Family-o'-Love.* Dutch sixteenth-century sect whose English advocates
   were prosecuted as heretical for practising free love and denying the
   immortality of the soul. Mary Faugh and Mulligrub of *The Dutch
   Courtesan* (Marston, 1605) belonged to this sect. cf. Middleton's
   Family of Love (*c.* 1602–07), in Bullen (ed.), *The Works of Thomas
   Middleton* (London, 1885–86), III, 3–5.

GOLDING

I believe you, Master Wolf. Good faith, sir, here's a great
deal of humility i' these letters.

WOLF

Humility, sir? Ay, were your worship an eye-witness of it,
you would say so. The knight will i' the Knight's Ward, do
what we can sir; and Master Quicksilver would be i' the   40
Hole if we would let him. I never knew or saw prisoners
more penitent, or more devout. They will sit you up all
night singing of psalms and edifying the whole prison. Only
Security sings a note too high sometimes, because he lies i'
the two-penny ward, far off, and cannot take his tune. The   45
neighbours cannot rest for him, but come every morning to
ask what godly prisoners we have.

TOUCHSTONE

Which on 'em is't is so devout—the knight, or the tother?

WOLF

Both, sir; but the young man especially! I never heard his
like! He has cut his hair too. He is so well given, and has   50
such good gifts. He can tell you almost all the stories of the
Book of Martyrs, and speak you all the Sick Man's Salve,
without book.

TOUCHSTONE

Ay, if he had had grace—he was brought up where it grew,
I wis. On, Master Wolf!   55

WOLF

And he has converted one Fangs, a sergeant, a fellow could
neither write nor read, he was called the Bandog o' the

---

53 *without book* by heart

39–45 *the Knight's Ward ... the Hole ... the two-penny ward.* The
    Counter had four types of accommodation, ranging in price from the
    Knight's Ward down to the Hole. See 'The Counter's Commonwealth'
    in Judges, op. cit., pp. 423–87, and *Westward Ho!* (ed. Bowers), III, ii,
    77–9. See above, note II, iii, 44.
50 *cut his hair.* i.e., from the courtier's length.
52 *Book of Martyrs.* John Foxe's famous classic, first published by John
    Day in 1561.
52 *Sick Man's Salve.* Thomas Becon's popular devotional prayers, sub-
    titled 'wherein all faithful Christians may learn both how to behave
    themselves patiently and thankfully in the time of sickness, and also
    vertuously to dispose their temporal goods, and finally prepare them-
    selves gladly and godly to die' (1561).
57 *Bandog.* Guard dog which had to be tied up because of its ferocity.

Counter; and he has brought him already to pare his nails,
and say his prayers; and 'tis hoped he will sell his place
shortly, and become an intelligencer.   60

TOUCHSTONE

No more; I am coming already. If I should give any farther
ear, I were taken. Adieu, gcod Master Wolf! Son, I do feel
mine own weaknesses; do not importune me. Pity is a rheum
that I am subject to; but I will resist it. Master Wolf, 'fish is
cast away that is cast in dry pools'. Tell Hypocrisy it will not   65
do; I have touched and tried too often; I am yet proof, and
I will remain so; when the Sessions come, they shall hear
from me. In the meantime, to all suits, to all entreaties, to
all letters, to all tricks, I will be deaf as an adder, and blind
as a beetle, lay mine ear to the ground, and lock mine eyes   70
i' my hand against all temptations.   *Exit*

GOLDING

You see, Master Wolf, how inexorable he is. There is no
hope to recover him. Pray you commend me to my brother
knight, and to my fellow Francis; present 'em with this small
token of my love [*Giving money*]. Tell 'em, I wish I could   75
do 'em any worthier office; but in this, 'tis desperate; yet
I will not fail to try the uttermost of my power for 'em. And,
sir, as far as I have any credit with you, pray you let 'em want
nothing; though I am not ambitious, they should know so
much.   80

WOLF

Sir, both your actions and words speak you to be a true
gentleman. They shall know only what is fit, and no more.
                                                      Exeunt

60 *intelligencer* informer
61 *coming* yielding
64–5 *fish is cast away*, etc. proverbial. Tilley, F307
66 *proof* impervious, invulnerable
79 *ambitious* eager, keen

---

66 *I have touched . . . too often.* Alchemical; mercury 'worked upon' the
   touchstone has been found wanting, and Touchstone, as a goldsmith,
   has 'tried' to change Quicksilver's nature.
69 *deaf as an adder*, etc. Refers to a belief that the adder stopped one ear
   with his tail and put the other to the ground, to deafen himself to the
   snakecharmer's music. cf. Psalm 58, 4. Proverbial. Tilley, A32.

[Act V, Scene iii
The Counter]

HOLDFAST, BRAMBLE

HOLDFAST
Who would you speak with, sir?

BRAMBLE
I would speak with one Security, that is prisoner here.

HOLDFAST
You are welcome, sir! Stay there, I'll call him to you. Master
Security!

SECURITY
[*At the grate*] Who calls?   5

HOLDFAST
Here's a gentleman would speak with you.

SECURITY
What is he? Is't one that grafts my forehead now I am in
prison, and comes to see how the horns shoot up and
prosper?

HOLDFAST
You must pardon him, sir; the old man is a little crazed with   10
his imprisonment.

SECURITY
What say you to me, sir? Look you here. My learned counsel,
Master Bramble! Cry you mercy, sir! When saw you my
wife?

BRAMBLE
She is now at my house, sir; and desired me that I would   15
come to visit you, and inquire of you your case, that we might
work some means to get you forth.

SECURITY
My case, Master Bramble, is stone walls and iron grates;
you see it, this is the weakest part on't. And, for getting me
forth, no means but hang myself, and so to be carried forth,   20
from which they have here bound me in intolerable bands.

1 s.d. HOLDFAST, BRAMBLE ed. (*Holdfast, Bramble; Security* Q)
16 *case* both encasement (i.e., prison) and a legal case

---

5 s.d. *At the grate.* Probably a lattice in one of the stage-doors as in
Marston's *Antonio's Revenge*, ed. G. K. Hunter (London, 1966), II, ii,
123. At V, iii, 18 Security complains of the 'iron grates' and at line 29
Quicksilver says 'the light does him harm', implying that the door or
trap could be closed to obscure him from vision. I am not altogether convinced by Irwin Smith's theory that Security appears at a 'window stage'
(*Shakespeare's Blackfriars Playhouse Its History and Its Design*, N.Y.,
1964, pp. 379–80).

BRAMBLE
Why, but what is't you are in for, sir?

SECURITY
For my sins, for my sins, sir, whereof marriage is the
greatest! O, had I never married, I had never known this
purgatory, to which hell is a kind of cool bath in respect.   25
My wife's confederacy, sir, with old Touchstone, that she
might keep her jubilee and the feast of her new moon. Do
you understand me, sir?

Enter QUICKSILVER

QUICKSILVER
Good sir, go in and talk with him. The light does him harm,
and his example will be hurtful to the weak prisoners. Fie,   30
Father Security, that you'll be still so profane! Will nothing
humble you?   [*Exeunt*]

Enter TWO PRISONERS *with a* FRIEND

FRIEND
What's he?

1 PRISONER
O, he is a rare young man! Do you not know him?

FRIEND
Not I! I never saw him, I can remember.   35

2 PRISONER
Why, it is he that was the gallant prentice of London—
Master Touchstone's man.

FRIEND
Who, Quicksilver?

1 PRISONER
Ay, this is he.

FRIEND
Is this he? They say he has been a gallant indeed.   40

1 PRISONER
O' the royalest fellow that ever was bred up i' the city! He
would play you his thousand pound a night at dice; keep
knights and lords company; go with them to bawdy-houses;
and his six men in a livery; kept a stable of hunting-horses,
and his wench in her velvet gown and her cloth of silver.   45
Here's one knight with him here in prison.

---

25 *in respect* by comparison

---

27 *her jubilee . . . new moon.* Celebration of cuckoldry, the crescent moon
being the symbol of the cuckold's horns.

FRIEND

And how miserably he is changed!

1 PRISONER

O, that's voluntary in him: he gave away all his rich clothes
as soon as ever he came in here among the prisoners; and
will eat o' the basket, for humility.   50

FRIEND

Why will he do so?

1 PRISONER

Alas, he has no hope of life! He mortifies himself. He does
but linger on till the Sessions.

2 PRISONER

O, he has penned the best thing, that he calls his 'Repentance'
or his 'Last Farewell', that ever you heard. He is a pretty   55
poet, and for prose—you would wonder how many prisoners
he has helped out, with penning petitions for 'em, and not
take a penny. Look! This is the knight, in the rug gown.
Stand by!

Enter PETRONEL, BRAMBLE, QUICKSILVER

BRAMBLE

Sir, for Security's case, I have told him. Say he should be   60
condemned to be carted or whipped for a bawd, or so; why,
I'll lay an execution on him o' two hundred pound; let him
acknowledge a judgement, he shall do it in half an hour; they
shall not all fetch him out without paying the execution, o'
my word.   65

PETRONEL

But can we not be bailed, Master Bramble?

BRAMBLE

Hardly; there are none of the judges in town, else you should
remove yourself (in spite of him) with a *habeas corpus*. But
if you have a friend to deliver your tale sensibly to some

---

56 *wonder* be surprised   60 s.d. (*Wolf* omit ed.)

---

50 *the basket.* The alms basket on which poor prisoners depended for their
     food, when staying in the Hole.
58 *rug gown.* The equivalent of sackcloth; worn by the penitent (H. & S.,
     IX, 676).
62 *lay an execution.* To allay or prevent the execution of sentence by
     putting down a bond: i.e., on a bond of £200 made out to Touchstone,
     if he agreed to drop the charge.
68 *habeas corpus.* i.e., by invoking this statute they would be moved to a
     different court and in the process might escape.

justice o' the town, that he may have feeling of it (do you   70
see) you may be bailed; for as I understand the case, 'tis
only done *in terrorem*; and you shall have an action of false
imprisonment against him when you come out, and perhaps
a thousand pound costs.

Enter MASTER WOLF

QUICKSILVER
How now, Master Wolf? What news? What return?   75
WOLF
Faith, bad all! Yonder will be no letters received. He says
the Sessions shall determine it. Only Master Deputy
Golding commends him to you, and with this token wishes
he could do you other good.

[*Gives money*]

QUICKSILVER
I thank him. Good Master Bramble, trouble our quiet no   80
more; do not molest us in prison thus with your winding
devices. Pray you, depart. For my part, I commit my cause
to him that can succour me; let God work his will. Master
Wolf, I pray you let this be distributed among the prisoners,
and desire 'em to pray for us.   85
WOLF
It shall be done, Master Francis.

[*Exit* QUICKSILVER]

1 PRISONER
An excellent temper!
2 PRISONER
Now God send him good luck!

Exeunt [BRAMBLE, TWO PRISONERS, *and* FRIEND]

PETRONEL
But what said my father-in-law, Master Wolf?

Enter HOLDFAST

HOLDFAST
Here's one would speak with you, sir.   90
WOLF
I'll tell you anon, Sir Petronel. Who is't?
HOLDFAST
A gentleman, sir, that will not be seen.

Enter GOLDING

82 *part* Q2 (pat Q1)

72 *in terrorem.* In fear, i.e., that he was blackmailed.

WOLF

Where is he? Master Deputy! Your worship is welcome—

GOLDING

Peace!

WOLF

Away, sirrah!   95

[Exit HOLDFAST *with* SIR PETRONEL]

GOLDING

Good faith, Master Wolf, the estate of these gentlemen, for
whom you were so late and willing a suitor, doth much
affect me; and because I am desirous to do them some fair
office, and find there is no means to make my father relent
so likely as to bring him to be a spectator of their miseries,   100
I have ventured on a device, which is, to make myself your
prisoner, entreating you will presently go report it to my
father, and (feigning an action, at suit of some third person)
pray him by this token [*Giving a ring*], that he will presently,
and with all secrecy, come hither for my bail; which train,   105
if any, I know will bring him abroad; and then, having him
here, I doubt not but we shall be all fortunate in the event.

WOLF

Sir, I will put on my best speed to effect it. Please you, come
in.

GOLDING

Yes; and let me rest concealed, I pray you.   110

WOLF

See here a benefit truly done, when it is done timely, freely,
and to no ambition.   *Exit* [*with* GOLDING]

[Act V, Scene iv

A Room in TOUCHSTONE's *House*]

Enter TOUCHSTONE, WIFE, DAUGHTERS, SINDEFY, WINIFRED

TOUCHSTONE

I will sail by you and not hear you, like the wise Ulysses.

MILDRED

Dear father!

MISTRESS TOUCHSTONE

Husband!

---

1 *Ulysses.* Ulysses sailed past the islands on which the sirens were singing
and stuffed his ears with wax until he was out of hearing.

GERTRUDE
  Father!
WINIFRED ⎱
SINDEFY ⎰
  Master Touchstone!   5
TOUCHSTONE
  Away, sirens, I will immure myself against your cries, and
  lock myself up to your lamentations.
MISTRESS TOUCHSTONE
  Gentle husband, hear me!
GERTRUDE
  Father, it is I, father, my Lady Flash. My sister and I am
  friends.   10
MILDRED
  Good father!
WINIFRED
  Be not hardened, good Master Touchstone!
SINDEFY
  I pray you, sir, be merciful!
TOUCHSTONE
  I am deaf, I do not hear you. I have stopped mine ears with
  shoemakers' wax, and drunk Lethe and mandragora to   15
  forget you. All you speak to me I commit to the air.

Enter WOLF

MILDRED
  How now, Master Wolf?
WOLF
  Where's Master Touchstone? I must speak with him pres-
  ently—I have lost my breath for haste.
MILDRED
  What's the matter, sir? Pray all be well!   20
WOLF
  Master Deputy Golding is arrested upon an execution, and
  desires him presently to come to him, forthwith.
MILDRED
  Ay me! Do you hear, father?

---

15 *shoemakers' wax*. An apt updating of the myth, and perhaps a sly dig at
    Dekker's *The Shoemakers' Holiday* in the pun on air (Ayre Q) in the
    next line, i.e., Simon Eyre.
15 *Lethe*. River of oblivion.
15 *mandragora*. Mandrake, a narcotic used to induce deep sleep.

TOUCHSTONE
Tricks, tricks, confederacy, tricks! I have 'em in my nose—
I scent 'em!   25
WOLF
Who's that? Master Touchstone?
MISTRESS TOUCHSTONE
Why, it is Master Wolf himself, husband.
MILDRED
Father!
TOUCHSTONE
I am deaf still, I say. I will neither yield to the song of the
siren, nor the voice of the hyena, the tears of the crocodile,   30
nor the howling o' the wolf. Avoid my habitation, monsters!
WOLF
Why, you are not mad, sir? I pray you, look forth, and see the
token I have brought you, sir.
TOUCHSTONE
Ha! What token is it?
WOLF
Do you know it, sir?   35
TOUCHSTONE
My son Golding's ring! Are you in earnest, Master Wolf?
WOLF
Ay, by my faith, sir! He is in prison, and required me to use
all speed and secrecy to you.
TOUCHSTONE
My cloak, there! Pray you be patient. I am plagued for my
austerity. My cloak! At whose suit, Master Wolf?   40
WOLF
I'll tell you as we go, sir.   *Exeunt*

[Act V, Scene v

The Counter]

Enter FRIEND, PRISONERS

FRIEND
Why, but is his offence such as he cannot hope of life?
1 PRISONER
Troth, it should seem so; and 'tis great pity, for he is exceeding penitent.

30 *hyena.* Topsell, *The History of the Four Footed Beasts* (1607), p. 437,
describes how the hyena earned his name as a counterfeiter. He could
supposedly mimic a man's cry, and thus lure searchers to their deaths.

FRIEND

They say he is charged but on suspicion of felony, yet.

2 PRISONER

Ay, but his master is a shrewd fellow; he'll prove great   5
matter against him.

FRIEND

I'd as lief as anything I could see his 'Farewell'.

1 PRISONER

O, 'tis rarely written; why, Toby may get him to sing it to
you; he's not curious to anybody.

2 PRISONER

O no! He would that all the world should take knowledge of   10
his 'Repentance', and thinks he merits in't, the more shame
he suffers.

1 PRISONER

Pray thee, try what thou canst do.

2 PRISONER

I warrant you, he will not deny it, if he be not hoarse with
the often repeating of it.   *Exit*   15

1 PRISONER

You never saw a more courteous creature than he is, and the
knight too: the poorest prisoner of the house may command
'em. You shall hear a thing admirably penned.

FRIEND

Is the knight any scholar too?

1 PRISONER

No, but he will speak very well, and discourse admirably of   20
running horses, and Whitefriars, and against bawds, and of
cocks; and talk as loud as a hunter, but is none.

Enter WOLF *and* TOUCHSTONE

WOLF

Please you, stay here, sir: I'll call his worship down to you.
                                                          [*Exit*]

Enter [2ND PRISONER *with*] QUICKSILVER, PETRONEL
[*and* SECURITY; GOLDING *with* WOLF, *who stands aside*]

9 *curious* particular, choosy
10 s.p. 2 PRISONER ed. (1 *Pris.* Q)
24 s.d. moved from line 26, ed. (*Enter Quick. Pet. &c.* Q)

---

21 *Whitefriars.* Sanctuary for debtors, later called Alsatia.

1 PRISONER

  See, he has brought him, and the knight too. Salute him, I
  pray. Sir, this gentleman, upon our report, is very desirous   25
  to hear some piece of your 'Repentance'.

QUICKSILVER

  Sir, with all my heart; and, as I told Master Toby, I shall be
  glad to have any man a witness of it. And the more openly I
  profess it, I hope it will appear the heartier and the more
  unfeigned.   30

TOUCHSTONE

  [*Aside*] Who is this? My man Francis, and my son-in-law?

QUICKSILVER

  Sir, it is all the testimony I shall leave behind me to the
  world, and my master, that I have so offended.

FRIEND

  Good sir!

QUICKSILVER

  I writ it when my spirits were oppressed.   35

PETRONEL

  Ay, I'll be sworn for you, Francis!

QUICKSILVER

  It is in imitation of Mannington's: he that was hanged at
  Cambridge, that cut off the horse's head at a blow.

FRIEND

  So, sir!

QUICKSILVER

  To the tune of, 'I wail in woe, I plunge in pain'.   40

---

  37 *Mannington's*. *Mannington's Repentance* is entered in the Stationers'
  Register, 7 November 1576, and described as 'a woeful ballad made by
  Mr. George Mannington an hour before he suffered [death] at
  Cambridge Castle' (for armed robbery). It is included in Clement
  Robinson's *A Handful of Pleasant Delights* (1584; ed. Arber, 1880,
  pp. 57–9). A different version appears in J. Ritson's *Ancient Songs and
  Ballads*, ed. W. C. Hazlitt (London, 1877), pp. 188–91. Hence, there is
  no reason to accept Charles Edmonds's suggestion, *Athenaeum*, 13
  October 1883, pp. 463–4, that Quicksilver's 'Repentance' is sketched
  from Luke Hutton's *The Black Dog of Newgate* (1596), or that Quicksilver is modelled on that figure. Doggerel repentances were, after all,
  extremely popular in Jacobean times.

  40 *I wail in woe ... pain*. The first lines of Mannington's *Repentance*.
  Quicksilver's song is a parody of the 'neck verses' sung by criminals on
  their way to the gallows at Tyburn.

PETRONEL
  An excellent ditty it is, and worthy of a new tune.
QUICKSILVER
  In Cheapside, famous for gold and plate,
  Quicksilver, I did dwell of late.
  I had a master good and kind,
  That would have wrought me to his mind.   45
  He bade me still, 'Work upon that',
  But, alas, I wrought I knew not what!
  He was a Touchstone black, but true,
  And told me still what would ensue;
  Yet, woe is me! I would not learn;   50
  I saw, alas, but could not discern!
FRIEND
  Excellent, excellent well!
GOLDING
  [*Aside to* WOLF] O, let him alone; he is taken already.
QUICKSILVER
  I cast my coat and cap away,
  I went in silks and satins gay;   55
  False metal of good manners, I
  Did daily coin unlawfully.
  I scorned my master, being drunk;
  I kept my gelding and my punk;
  And with a knight, Sir Flash by name,   60
  (Who now is sorry for the same)—
PETRONEL
  I thank you, Francis!
QUICKSILVER
  I thought by sea to run away,
  But Thames and tempest did me stay.
TOUCHSTONE
  [*Aside*] This cannot be feigned, sure. Heaven pardon my   65
  severity! The ragged colt may prove a good horse.
GOLDING
  [*Aside*] How he listens, and is transported! He has forgot me.

---

53 *is taken* either understood or, more probably, has begun
56 *False metal* i.e., counterfeit
66 *The ragged colt . . . horse* proverbial. Tilley, C522

---

48 *Touchstone black, but true.* Refers to the property of dark quartz (touchstone) to reveal the true nature of the metals 'worked' against it.

untitled

QUICKSILVER
Still Eastward Ho was all my word;
But westward I had no regard,
Nor never thought what would come after,   70
As did, alas, his youngest daughter!
At last the black ox trod o' my foot,
And I saw then what 'longed unto't.
Now cry I, 'Touchstone, touch me still,
And make me current by thy skill'.   75

TOUCHSTONE
[*Aside*] And I will do it, Francis.

WOLF
[*Aside to* GOLDING] Stay him, Master Deputy; now is [not] the time; we shall lose the song else.

FRIEND
I protest, it is the best that ever I heard.

QUICKSILVER
How like you it, gentlemen?   80

ALL
O, admirable, sir!

QUICKSILVER
This stanze now following alludes to the story of Mannington, from whence I took my project for my invention.

FRIEND
Pray you, go on, sir.

QUICKSILVER
O Mannington, thy stories show,   85
Thou cut'st a horse-head off at a blow!
But I confess, I have not the force
For to cut off the head of a horse;
Yet I desire this grace to win,

off

77–8 *now is not the time* ed. (now is the time Q)
83 *project* model

---

71 *his youngest daughter* i.e., Mildred (I, i, 74–81). Not strictly true since Touchstone (I, i, 95–6) and Golding (I, i, 132–6) predict his downfall. Probably used because the form 'dafter' rhymes with 'after'.
72 *black ox.* Symbol of adversity. Proverbial. Tilley, O 103.
74 *touch me still.* i.e., continue to test me and reveal my true value.
75 *make me current.* Quicksilver (who has become false metal) wishes Touchstone to convert him back to current (true) metal; i.e., silver or gold that is genuine.

That I may cut off the horse-head of Sin,   90
And leave his body in the dust
Of Sin's highway and bogs of Lust,
Whereby I may take Virtue's purse,
And live with her for better, for worse.

FRIEND
Admirable, sir, and excellently conceited!   95
QUICKSILVER
Alas, sir!
TOUCHSTONE
[*Coming to* GOLDING *and* WOLF] Son Golding and Master
Wolf, I thank you: the deceit is welcome, especially from
thee, whose charitable soul in this hath shown a high point
of wisdom and honesty. Listen! I am ravished with his   100
'Repentance', and could stand here a whole prenticeship to
hear him.
FRIEND
Forth, good sir!
QUICKSILVER
This is the last, and the 'Farewell'.

Farewell, Cheapside, farewell, sweet trade   105
Of goldsmiths all, that never shall fade!
Farewell, dear fellow prentices all,
And be you warned by my fall:
Shun usurers, bawds, and dice, and drabs;
Avoid them as you would French scabs.   110
Seek not to go beyond your tether,
But cut your thongs unto your leather;
So shall you thrive by little and little,
'Scape Tyburn, Counters, and the Spital!

103 *Forth* go on
110 *French scabs* syphilis

90–4 *That I may cut off the horse-head of Sin . . . purse.* i.e., like the high-
wayman he wishes to seize Virtue's purse by slaying the horse on which
she rides.
101 *whole prenticeship.* i.e., usually seven years.
112 *cut . . . leather.* Proverbial. Tilley, T229. The proverb is: 'It is not
honest to make large thongs of other men's leather'—i.e., to be lavish
with that which is another's. Hence Quicksilver is saying: 'live according
to your means', or, 'cut your coat according to your cloth'.
114 *Spital.* The general term for a charitable institution for the poor,
specializing in the treatment of venereal diseases.

6

TOUCHSTONE
And scape them shalt thou, my penitent and dear Francis!   115
QUICKSILVER
Master!
PETRONEL
Father!
TOUCHSTONE
I can no longer forbear to do your humility right. Arise, and
let me honour your 'Repentance' with the hearty and joyful
embraces of a father and friend's love. Quicksilver, thou hast   120
eat into my breast, Quicksilver, with the drops of thy sorrow,
and killed the desperate opinion I had of thy reclaim.
QUICKSILVER
O, sir, I am not worthy to see your worshipful face!
PETRONEL
Forgive me, father!
TOUCHSTONE
Speak no more! All former passages are forgotten, and here   125
my word shall release you. Thank this worthy brother and
kind friend, Francis.—Master Wolf, I am their bail.

                           A shout in the prison
               [SECURITY *appears at the grate*]

SECURITY
Master Touchstone! Master Touchstone!
TOUCHSTONE
Who's that?
WOLF
Security, sir.   130
SECURITY
Pray you, sir, if you'll be won with a song, hear my lament-
able tune, too!

                          SONG
               O Master Touchstone,
               My heart is full of woe!
               Alas, I am a cuckold;   135
               And why should it be so?

122 *reclaim* i.e., reclamation, conversion
125 *passages* events, happenings

120–1 *Quicksilver, thou hast eat into my breast.* Refers to mercury's charac-
    teristic property of dissolving gold; Touchstone's heart of gold is
    easily overcome.

Because I was a usurer,
And bawd, as all you know,
For which, again I tell you,
My heart is full of woe.   140

TOUCHSTONE

Bring him forth, Master Wolf, and release his bands. This
day shall be sacred to Mercy and the mirth of this encounter
in the Counter—see, we are encountered with more suitors!

Enter MISTRESS TOUCHSTONE, GERTRUDE, MILDRED,
SINDEFY, WINIFRED, &c.

Save your breath, save your breath! All things have succeeded to your wishes, and we are heartily satisfied in their   145
events.

GERTRUDE

Ah, runaway, runaway! Have I caught you? And how has
my poor Knight done all this while?

PETRONEL

Dear Lady-wife, forgive me.

GERTRUDE

As heartily as I would be forgiven, Knight. Dear father, give   150
me your blessing, and forgive me too. I ha' been proud and
lascivious, father, and a fool, father; and being raised to the
state of a wanton coy thing, called a lady, father, have
scorned you, father, and my sister, and my sister's velvet
cap, too; and would make a mouth at the City as I rid   155
through it; and stop mine ears at Bow-bell. I have said your
beard was a base one, father; and that you looked like
Twierpipe the taborer; and that my mother was but my
midwife.

MISTRESS TOUCHSTONE

Now God forgi' you, Child Madam!   160

TOUCHSTONE

No more repetitions! What is else wanting to make our
harmony full?

GOLDING

Only this, sir: that my fellow Francis make amends to
Mistress Sindefy with marriage.

---

158 *Twierpipe the taborer.* Tabor = a small drum, usually played in con-
junction with a pipe and singing. H. & S., IX, 677, note: 'Tweire-pipe
that famous Southern Taberer with the Cowleyan windpipe, who for
whuling hath beene famous through the Globe of the world'. From the
anonymous tract *Old Meg of Herefordshire* (1609), Dedication.

QUICKSILVER

With all my heart!   165

GOLDING

And Security give her a dower, which shall be all the restitu-
tion he shall make of that huge mass he hath so unlawfully
gotten.

TOUCHSTONE

Excellently devised! A good motion! What says Master
Security?   170

SECURITY

I say anything, sir, what you'll ha' me say. Would I were no
cuckold!

WINIFRED

Cuckold, husband? Why, I think this wearing of yellow has
infected you.

TOUCHSTONE

Why, Master Security, that should rather be a comfort to   175
you than a corrosive. If you be a cuckold, it's an argument
you have a beautiful woman to your wife; then, you shall be
much made of; you shall have store of friends; never want
money; you shall be eased of much o' your wedlock pain:
others will take it for you. Besides, you being a usurer, and   180
likely to go to hell, the devils will never torment you; they'll
take you for one o' their own race. Again, if you be a cuckold,
and know it not, you are an innocent; if you know it and
endure it, a true martyr.

SECURITY

I am resolved, sir. Come hither, Winny!   185

TOUCHSTONE

Well, then, all are pleased; or shall be anon. Master Wolf,
you look hungry, methinks; have you no apparel to lend
Francis to shift him?

QUICKSILVER

No, sir, nor I desire none; but here make it my suit, that I

---

188 *shift him* enable him to change his clothes

173–4 *wearing of yellow*, etc. i.e., the colour of jealousy (cf. Malvolio in
        Twelfth Night).
176–80 *If you . . . for you*. Closely parallels Rabelais, *Gargantua and Panta-
        gruel*, III, chapter xxvii—see trans. T. Urquhart and P. Le Motteux,
        3 vols. (London, 1934), II, 135–6. See also, A. J. Farmer, op. cit., p. 325.
176 *corrosive*. Indicates the properties of sulphur, which is precipitated from
        the alchemical solution, just as Security is here cast out of society.
183 *innocent*. With a probable play on the meaning 'idiot' or 'cretin'.

may go home through the streets in these, as a spectacle, or   190
rather an example, to the children of Cheapside.

TOUCHSTONE

Thou hast thy wish. Now, London, look about,
And in this moral see thy glass run out:
Behold the careful father, thrifty son,
The solemn deeds which each of us have done;   195
The usurer punished, and from fall so steep
The prodigal child reclaimed, and the lost sheep.

---

193 *glass* i.e., hourglass; fig. time

192–7 *Thou hast ... sheep.* Reminiscent of the thumping moral verse of
such earlier prodigal son dramas as *Liberality and Prodigality*, presented
at Blackfriars in 1601.

EPILOGUE

[QUICKSILVER]

Stay, sir, I perceive the multitude are gathered together to view our coming out at the Counter. See, if the streets and the fronts of the houses be not stuck with people, and the windows filled with ladies, as on the solemn day of the Pageant!   5

O may you find in this our pageant, here,
The same contentment which you came to seek,
And as that show but draws you once a year,
May this attract you hither once a week.   [*Exeunt*]

FINIS

---

3 *stuck* i.e., stuck full, jammed
9 s.d. moved from line 197, ed.

---

1 s.p. Like Dodsley and other eds., I assign this speech to Quicksilver.
2 *the streets and the fronts of the houses*. Probably referring to the audience: *the streets*, i.e., those seated on benches in the pit; *the fronts of the houses*, i.e., the galleries and boxes. See Gurr, op. cit., p. 105.
9 *once a week*. Plays were usually performed weekly (on Saturday), in the private theatres.

APPENDIX 1

Map of London, Westminster and Southwark, with views on the river from Greenwich to Gravesend. By J. Moor circa 1662. (B. M. Crace Collection Catalogue, Portfolio I.44.)

Printed by kind permission of the Trustees of the British Museum.

Essex.

Borve

Borve Creeke

Borve

East Indiahouse

Stepney

Popler

Limehouse

Breach

Cuckolds Haven

Kings Medowe

Blackwall Marsh

Greenwich Marish

Redriffe

Lime house Reach

Blackwall Reach

Ileof Dogs

St Cripe

Halfeway house

Greenwich Reach

the Kings yard

Greenwich

Deptford

Depfo Creeke

APPENDIX 2

This anonymous ballad found in B.M. Addit. Mss. 5, 832, fol. 205 is entitled 'Verses upon the order for the making Knights of such persons who had £40 per annum, in King James the First's time'. I include it because it so perfectly describes the mood of the country after James resorted to selling knighthoods to raise money. According to John Philipot, in his *Perfect Collection or Catalogue of all Knights Batchelours made by King James, since his coming to the Crown of England* (1660), James I created 2,323 knights, of whom 900 were made the first year of his reign (1603).[1] One of these knights was Sir James Murray (knighted 5 August 1603), who apparently informed the king of the political satire in *Eastward Ho!* He may have felt the well aimed barb at IV, i, 167–71:

1 GENTLEMAN
  I ken the man weel, he's one of my thirty-pound knights.
2 GENTLEMAN
  No, no, this is he that stole his knighthood o'the grand day for four pound, giving to a page all the money in's purse, I wot well.

Come all you farmers out of the country,
Carters, ploughmen, hedgers, and all;
Tom, Dick and Will, Ralph, Roger, and Humphrey,
Leave off your gestures rustical.
Bid all your home-spun russets adieu,
And suit yourself in fashions new;
Honour invites you to delights—
Come all to Court, and be made Knights.

He that hath forty pounds per annum
Shall be promoted from the plough;
His wife shall take the wall of her grannum,
Honour is sold so dog-cheap now.
Though thou hast neither good birth nor breeding,
If thou hast money thou'rt sure of speeding.
Honour invites you , &c.

[1] W. Chappell, *Popular Music of Olden Time*, 2 vols. (London, 1885–89), I, 326–7.

Knighthood, in old time, was counted an honour,
Which the blest spirits did not disdain;
But now it is used in so base a manner,
That it's no credit, but rather a stain.
Tush, it's no matter what people do say,
The name of a Knight a whole village will sway.
Honour invites you, &c.

Shepherds, leave singing your pastoral sonnets,
And to learn compliments show your endeavours;
Cast off for ever your two shilling bonnets,
Cover your coxcombs with three pound beavers.
Sell cart and tar-box, new coaches to buy,
Then, 'Good, your worship', the vulgar will cry.
Honour invites you, &c.

And thus unto worship being advanced,
Keep all your tenants in awe with your frowns,
And let your rents be yearly enhanced,
To buy your new-moulded madams new gowns.
Joan, Siss, and Nell, shall all be ladyfied,
Instead of hay-carts, in coaches shall ride.
Honour invites you, &c.

Whatever you do, have care of expenses;
In hospitality do not exceed;
Greatness of followers belongeth to princes,
A coachman and footman are all that you need.
And still observe this—let your servants meat lack,
To keep brave apparel upon your wife's back.
Honour invites you, &c.

APPENDIX 3

IMPRISONMENT

One of the most memorable episodes in Jonson's *Conversations with Drummond* is the story surrounding the *Eastward Ho!* imprisonment. He told Drummond:

> He was delated by Sir James Murray to the King for writing something against the Scots in a play Eastward Ho and voluntarily imprisoned himself with Chapman and Marston, who had written it amongst them. The report was that they should then [have] had their ears cut and noses. After their delivery he banqueted all his friends, there was Camden, Selden and others. At the midst of the feast his old mother drank to him and show[ed] him a paper which she had (if the sentence had taken execution) to have mixed in the prison among his drink, which was full of lusty strong poison and that she was no churl she told she minded first to have drunk of it herself.[2]

Besides this account, ten letters, three by Chapman and seven by Jonson, were discovered in a collection of seventeenth-century manuscripts owned by Mr T. A. White of New York. Bertram Dobell published them in the *Athenaeum*, 23, 30 March; 6, 13 April 1901 under the title 'Newly Discovered Elizabethan Documents'. On the basis of their content Dobell conjectured that the letters refer to *Eastward Ho!* and his conclusion is substantiated by Herford and Simpson (*Ben Jonson*, I, 191–3). Dobell thought that Chapman was the probable collector if not the actual scribe. One of the letters (*Jonson* B) is also found in holograph in the Cecil Papers 119, 58. (I have used copies of the letters as found in Schelling and Herford and Simpson, and modernized spelling and punctuation.)

The circumstances of the imprisonment related by Jonson in his conversations concur at several points with the letters. They are in prison because they have aroused 'his Majesty's high displeasure'; they are 'unexamined or unheard'; and the cause is 'not our own'. The letters do not, however, confirm Jonson's story of how he gave himself up nor do they explain the absence of Marston. Jonson's

---

[2] H. & S., I, 140 (here modernized).

continual plea that *Rumour* is not to be trusted favours the theory that unlicensed production was the actual cause of the offence. (See above, *Date and Sources*, p. xxiii–xxv.)

Whatever the cause, the imprisonment must have been short-lived. Evidently their patrons secured a rapid release. *Chapman* III mentions that D'Aubigny has intervened on behalf of Jonson. We know that Jonson attended a party given by Robert Catesby, a conspirator in the Gunpowder Plot, on 9 October 1605.[3]

I

To His Most Gracious Majesty.

Vouchsafe most excellent Sovereign to take merciful notice of the submissive and amendful sorrows of your two most humble and prostrated subjects for your Highness' displeasure: Geo: Chapman and Ben Jhonson; whose chief offences are but two clauses, and both of them not our own; much less the unnatural issue of our offence-less intents. I hope your Majesty's universal knowledge will deign to remember that all authority in execution of justice especially respects the manners and lives of men commanded before it; and according to their general actions censures anything that hath 'scaped them in particular; which cannot be so disproportionable that one being actually good, the other should be intentionally ill, if not intentionally (howsoever it may lie subject to construction)—where the whole fount of our actions may be justified from being in this kind offensive—I hope the integral parts will taste of the same loyal and dutiful order: which to aspire from your most Caesar-like bounty (who conquered still to spare the conquered, and was glad of offences that he might forgive). In all dejection of never-enough iterated sorrow for your high displeasure, and vow of as much future delight as of your present anger; we cast our best parts at your Highness' feet, and our worst to hell.

GEORGE CHAPMAN.

II

To The Most Worthy and Honourable Protector of Virtue: The Lord Chamberlain.

Most Worthily Honoured:

Of all the oversights for which I suffer none repents me so much as that our unhappy book was presented without your Lordship's

[3] ibid., XI, 578.

allowance. For which we can plead nothing by way of pardon, but your Person so far removed from our required attendance; our play so much importuned; and our clear opinions that nothing it contained could worthily be held offensive. And had your good Lordship vouchsafed this addition of grace to your late free bounties, to have heard our reasons for our well weighed opinions; and the words truly related on which both they and our enemies' complaints were grounded, I make no question but your impartial justice would have stood much further from their clamour than from our acquittal. Which indifferent favour, if yet your no less than princely respect of virtue shall please to bestow on her poor observant and command my appearance; I doubt not but the tempest that hath driven me into this wrackful harbour will clear with my innocence: and withal the most sorrow-inflicting wrath of his excellent Majesty; which to my most humble and zealous affection is so much the more stormy, by how much some of my obscured labours have strived to aspire instead thereof his illustrate favour; and shall not be the least honour to his most Royal virtues.

GEORGE CHAPMAN.

III

[To The Earl of Suffolk:The Lord Chamberlain.]

Notwithstanding your Lordship's infinite free bounty hath pardoned and graced when it might justly have punished; and remembered our poor reputations when our acknowledged duties to your Lordship might worthily seem forgotten; yet since true honour delights to increase with increase of goodness; and that our abilities and healths faint under our irksome burdens; we are with all humility enforced to solicit the propagation of your most noble favours to our present freedom: and the rather since we hear from Lord D'Awbney, that his Highness hath remitted one of us wholly to your Lordship's favour. And that the other had still your Lordship's passing noble remembrance for his joint liberty; which his Highness' self would not be displeased to allow. And thus with all gratitude admiring your no less than sacred respect to the poor estate of virtue, never were our souls more appropriate to the powers of our lives, than our utmost lives are consecrate to your noblest service.

GEORGE CHAPMAN.

A

[To An Unnamed Lord, probably The Earl of Suffolk, 1605.[4]]
Most Honourable Lord:

Although I cannot but know your Lordship to be busied with far greater and higher affairs than to have leisure to descend suddenly on an estate so low and removed as mine; yet since the cause is in us wholly mistaken (at least misconstrued), and that every noble and just man is bound to defend the innocent; I doubt not but to find your Lordship full of that wonted virtue and favour; wherewith you have ever abounded toward the truth. And though the imprisonment itself cannot but grieve me (in respect of his Majesty's high displeasure, from whence it proceeds) yet the manner of it afflicts me more being committed hither, unexamined, nay unheard (a right not commonly denied to the greatest offenders), and I made a guilty man, long before I am one, or ever thought to be. God I call to testimony what my thoughts are and ever have been of his Majesty; and so may I thrive when he comes to be my judge and my King's, as they are most sincere.

And I appeal to posterity that will hereafter read and judge my writings (though now neglected) whether it be possible I should speak of his Majesty as I have done, without the affection of a most zealous and good subject. It hath ever been my destiny to be misreported and condemned on the first tale; but I hope there is an ear left for me, and by your honour I hope it, who have always been friend to justice; a virtue that crowns your nobility. So with my most humble prayer of your pardon, and all advanced wishes for your honour, I begin to know my duty, which is to forbear to trouble your Lordship till my languishing estate may draw free breath from your comfortable word.

BEN: JOHNSON.

B

To The Most Nobly-Virtuous and Thrice-Honoured Earl of Salisbury,[5] 1605.

Most Truly Honourable,/

It hath still been the tyranny of my fortune so to oppress my endeavours that before I can show myself grateful in the least for former benefits, I am enforced to provoke your bounties for more. May it not seem grievous to your Lordship that now my innocence

[4] ibid., I, 194.
[5] Created Earl of Salisbury on 5 May 1605.

calls upon you (next the Deity) to her defence—God himself is not averted at just men's cries—and you, that approach that divine goodness and supply it here on earth in your place and honours, cannot employ your aids more worthily than to the commune succour of honesty and virtue, how humbly soever it be placed.

I am here, my most honoured Lord, unexamined or unheard, committed to a vile prison, and with me a gentleman (whose name may perhaps have come to your Lordship), one Mr. *George Chapman*, a learned and honest man. The cause (would I could name some worthier, though I wish we had known none worthy our imprisonment), is (the word irks me that our fortune hath necessitated us to so despised a course), a play, my Lord; whereof we hope there is no man can justly complain that hath the virtue to think but favourably of himself; if our judge bring an equal ear, marry, if with prejudice we be made guilty afore our time, we must embrace the asinine virtue, patience./ My noble Lord, they deal not charitably who are too witty in another man's works, and utter sometimes their own malicious meanings under our words. I protest to your honour, and call God to testimony (since my first error, which yet is punished in me more with my shame than it was then with my bondage),[6] I have so attempered my style, that I have given no cause to any good man of grief, and if to any ill, by touching at any general vice, it hath always been with a regard and sparing of particular persons. I may be otherwise reported; but if all that be accused should be presently guilty, there are few men would stand in the state of innocence./

I beseech your most honourable Lordship, suffer not other men's errors or faults past to be made my crimes; but let me be examined both by all my works past and this present; and not trust to *Rumour* but my books (for she is an unjust deliverer both of great and small actions), whether I have ever (in anything I have written, private, or public) given offence to a nation, to any public order or state, or any person of honour or authority; but have equally laboured to keep their dignity, as mine own person, safe. If others have transgressed, let not me be entitled to their follies. But lest in being too diligent for my excuse, I may incur the suspicion of being guilty, I become a most humble suitor to your Lordship that with the honourable Lord *Chamberlain* (to whom I have in like manner petitioned), you will be pleased to be the grateful means of our coming to answer; or if in your wisdoms it shall be thought unnecessary, that your Lordships will be the most honoured cause of

[6] i.e., Jonson's imprisonment for his share in Thomas Nashe's *The Isle of Dogs* (1597), for which he was tried by Salisbury (then Sir Robert Cecil).

our liberty, where freeing us from one prison you shall remove us
to another; which is eternally to bind us and our muses, to the
thankful honouring of you and yours to posterity; as your own
virtues have by many descents of ancestors ennobled you to time./
Your Honour's most devoted in heart as words./

BEN: JONSON.

C

[To an Unnamed Lord, 1605]

Noble Lord,
   I have so confirmed opinion of your virtue, and am so fortified
in mine own innocence, as I dare (without blushing at anything save
your trouble) put my fame into your hands, which I prefer to my
life. The cause of my commitment I understand is his Majesty's
high displeasure conceived against me; for which I am most inwardly
sorry; but how I should deserve it, I have yet, I thank God, so much
integrity as to doubt. If I have been misreported to his Majesty, the
punishment I now suffer may I hope merit more of his princely
favour, when he shall know me truly: every accusation doth not
condemn, and there must go much more to the making of a guilty
man, than rumour. I therefore crave of your Lordship this noble
benefit; rightly to inform his Majesty that I never in thought, word,
or act had purpose to offend or grieve him; but with all my powers
have studied to show myself most loyal and zealous to his whole
designs; that in private and public, by speech and writing, I have
ever professed it; and if there be one man or devil to be produced
that can affirm the contrary let me suffer under all extremity that
justice, nay tyranny, can inflict. I speak not this with any spirit of
contumacy, for I know there is no subject hath so safe an innocence
but may rejoice to stand justified in sight of his Sovereign's mercy.
To which we most humbly submit ourselves, our lives and fortunes.

BEN: JOHNSON.

D

[To An Unnamed Lady, probably The Countess of Bedford. 1605.[7]]

Excellentest of Ladies,
   And most honoured of the graces, muses, and me; if it be not a
sin to profane your free hand with prison polluted paper, I would
entreat some little of your aid to the defence of my innocence, which

[7] H. & S., I, 198. Schelling in his edition of *Eastward Ho!* conjectures that
the lady to whom this letter is addressed is the Countess of Rutland.

is as clear as this leaf was (before I stained it) of anything half-worthy this violent infliction. I am committed and with me a worthy friend, one Mr. Chapman, a man, I cannot say how known to your Ladyship, but I am sure known to me to honour you. And our offence a play, so mistaken, so misconstrued, so misapplied, as I do wonder whether their ignorance or impudence be most, who are our adversaries. It is now not disputable for we stand on uneven bases, and our cause so unequally carried, as we are—without examining, without hearing, or without any proof but malicious *Rumour*—hurried to bondage and fetters. The cause we understand to be the King's indignation, for which we are heartily sorry, and the more by how much the less we have deserved it. What our suit is, the worthy employed solicitor and equal adorer of your virtues, can best inform you.

BEN: JHONSON.

E

[To Esme, Lord D'Aubigny? 1605.[8]]

The noble favours you have done us, most worthy Lord, cannot be so concealed or removed but that they have broke in upon us even where we lie double bound to their comforts. Nor can we doubt, but he who hath so far and freely adventured to the relief of our virtue will go on to the utmost release of it. And though I know your Lordship hath been far from doing anything herein to your own ambition; yet be pleased to take this protestation, that, next his Majesty's favour, I shall not covet that thing more in the world than to express the lasting gratitude I have conceived in soul towards your Lordship.

BEN: JOHNSON.

F

[To The Earl of] Mon[t]gomerie[9]

Most Worthily Honoured,

For me not to solicit or call you to succour in a time of such need, were no less a sin of despair, than a neglect of your honour. Your power, your place, and readiness to do good invite me, and mine own cause (which shall never discredit the least of your favours) is a main encouragement. If I lay here on my desert, I should be the

---

[8] Jonson had been staying with D'Aubigny in 1603.
[9] Patron of the playwright Massinger. According to H. & S. also created earl on 5 May 1605.

more backward to importune you; but as it is (most worthy Earl) our offence being our misfortune, not our malice; I challenge your aid, as to the common defence of virtue; but more peculiarly to me, who have always in heart so particularly honoured you. I know it is now no time to boast affections, lest, while I sue for favours I should be thought to buy them; but if the future services of a man so removed to you and low in merit may aspire any place in your thoughts; let it lie upon the forfeiture of my humanity, if I omit the least occasion to express them. And so, not doubting of your noble endeavours to reflect his Majesty's most repented on our parts and sorrowed-for displeasure, I commit my fortune, reputation, and innocence into your most happy hands; and reiterated protestation of being ever most grateful.

BEN: JOHNSON.

G

[To The Earl of] Pembroke.

Most Noble Earl:

Neither am I or my cause so much unknown to your Lordship as it should drive me to seek a second means, or despair of this to your favour. You have ever been free and noble to me, and I doubt not the same proportion of your bounties, if I can but answer it with preservation of my virtue and innocence: when I fail of those let me not only be abandoned of you, but of men. 'The anger of the King is death', sayeth the wise man, and in truth it is little less with me and my friend; for it hath buried us quick. And though we know it only the property of men guilty, and worthy of punishment, to invoke *Mercy*; yet now it might relieve us, who have only our fortunes made our fault; and are indeed vexed for other men's licence. Most honoured Earl; be hasty to our succour, and it shall be our care and study not to have you repent the timely benefit you do us; which we will ever gratefully receive and multiply in our acknowledgement.

BEN: JOHNSON.

APPENDIX 4

First Quarto Press Corrections

More than two hundred corrections were made to the first quarto of *Eastward Ho!* as it passed through the press. Half of these are minor changes made when the cancel E3^r–E4^v (III, ii, 303–III, iii, 108) was reset in a censored form. The rest are minor variants in punctuation scattered throughout the text. Some of these may have been a result of editing in the press, others can be attributed to the compositors' faulty setting of copy.

Ten of the eleven copies were collated on the Bodleian Hinman collator, the Pforzheimer copy was collated from microfilm. The following copies were consulted:

The First Issue (a^i)

1	The Wise copy from the British Museum, Ashley 371.	(xerox)
9*	The E3^r–E4^v cancellandum included in the made-up Dyce copy from the Victoria and Albert Museum.	(xerox)

The Second Issue (a^{ii})

2	The Bodleian copy, Mal. 765.	(photograph)
3	The British Museum copy, C56 d32.	(photograph)
4	The Worcester College, Oxford, copy, Mal. 252.	(Q)
5	The M.I.T. copy.	(photograph)
6	The Folger copy.	(photograph)
7	The Yale copy.	(photograph)
8	The Huntington copy.	(photograph)
9	The Dyce copy in the Victoria and Albert Museum.	(xerox)
10	The Clark copy in the University of California, Los Angeles—gathering E is misarranged.	(xerox)
11	The Pforzheimer copy.	(microfilm)

In the following pages the numbers on the left are used to represent the copies.

Sig. A1ʳ & A1ᵛ in copy 1 have been substituted from Q3. On A1ʳ, 6, 'By' has a swash 'B' not present in Q1. The type used to set Prologus on A1ᵛ is that of Q3 not Q1.

Location						
I, i, 41	Whyi	9	Why?	the rest	Sig. A2ᵛ	15
Running Title *ASTWARED*		1, 7, 8, 11	*EASTWARED*	,,	Si. A3ʳ	
I, i, 76	Boy?	1, 7, 11	Boy.	,,	,,	17
I, ii, 21	smockes	1, 7, 11	smocks	,,	Sig. A4ᵛ	1
23	pipkines	,,	pipkins	,,	,,	3
23	bodkins:	,,	bodkins:—	,,	,,	3
48	Apes	,,	Ape's	,,	,,	29
56	Tailer.	1, 11	Tailer!	,,	Sig. B1ʳ	3
68	[final] there,	,,	there!	,,	,,	17
76	it is,	,,	it is:	,,	,,	25
81	*Baboone. Jesu.*	,,	*Baboone? Jesu!*	,,	,,	30
82	countrey	,,	countrey?	,,	,,	31
II, i, 63	evermore	,,	ever more	,,	Sig. B3ʳ	36
84	Am pum pull eo, Pullo; showse quot the Caliver.		(Ump) pulldo, Pulldo; showse quoth the Caliver.			
		3, 10		the rest	Sig. B3ᵛ	20
s.p. 146	*Con.*	1, 11	*Goul.*	,,	Sig. B4ᵛ	1
II, ii, 5	hords	,,	hoords	,,	,,	25
73	craft	1, 3, 10	craft,	,,	Sig. C1ᵛ	23
95	hundred,	,,	hundred:	,,	Sig. C2ʳ	12
96	perrill	,,	perill	,,	,,	13
116	be call me	,,	bee calme	,,	,,	34
II, iii, 52	Angell· to	1, 3, 10	Angell. To	,,	Sig. C4ʳ	32
52	too which	,,	to which	,,	,,	32
III, i, 10	some thing	7, 11	something	,,	Sig. D2ʳ	7
25	harts all	,,	hearts al	,,	,,	24
s.d. 38	*Enter a Messenger. Exit.*	,,	*Exit. Enter a Messenger.*	,,	,,	38
III, ii, s.d. 4	*Hawlet*	7, 11	*Hamlet*	,,	Sig. D3ʳ	1
s.d. 4	*hast.*	,,	*haste.*	,,	,,	1
s.p. 14, 17, 21, 24	*Gaze.*	,,	*Gaz.*	,,		15, 18, 22, 25
19	'ith;	,,	'ith'	,,	,,	20
35	it has	,,	it'has	,,	,,	37
52	Honny Suckle	,,	*Honny Suckle*	,,	Sig. D3ᵛ	18
58	*Quick.* Marry	,,	*Quick.* Mary	,,	,,	24
65	*Madam*	,,	*Madam,*	,,	,,	31
65	mary	,,	marry	,,	,,	31

	70	Lady	,,	Lady,	,,	,, 36
	72	*Quicksilver*	,,	*Quicksilver*	,,	,, 38
	133	to	,,	too	,,	Sig. D4ᵛ 22
	138	show:	,,	show.	,,	,, 28
	144	hast after	,,	haste after	,,	,, 33
	151	*Ladie*	,,	*Ladie,*	,,	,, 39
	182	ende—	1, 3, 11	ende!	,,	Sig. E1ʳ 34
	187	eude	,,	ende	,,	,, 39
	201	voyadge	1, 2, 3, 5, 11	voyage	,,	Sig. E1ᵛ 15
	203	yonr	,,	your	,,	,, 18
	216	enioy	,,	enioy	,,	,, 31
	218	*hunger!*	,,	*hunger*	,,	,, 33
III, ii,	225	sernice	1, 2, 3, 5, 11	seruice	,,	Sig. E2ʳ 1
	243	prettie	,,	pretie	,,	,, 19
	251	praisd'e	,,	prais'de	,,	,, 27
	257	eis	,,	his	,,	,, 33
	257	Ielosie	,,	Ielosie;	,,	,, 33
	261	To finde	,,	Two fine	,,	,, 37
	261	Beastes!	,,	Beastes	,,	,, 37
	261	Lawyer?	,,	Lawyer	,,	,, 37

Sig. E3ʳ R.T.		*HOE.*	1, 9*	*HOE*	the rest	
III, ii,	309	was	,,	shas	,,	Sig. E3ʳ 7
	310	Gentlemen!	,,	Gentlemen?	,,	,, 8
	311	Gossip:	,,	Gossip!	,,	,, 9
	314	now	,,	now—	,,	,, 11
	317	will	,,	wil	,,	,, 13
	318	[second] Why	,,	why	,,	,, 14
	325	wil	,,	will	,,	,, 20
	326	by'th	,,	by th'	,,	,, 21
	326	word,	,,	word	,,	,, 21
	331	waite	,,	wait	,,	,, 26
	331	sir,	,,	sir.	,,	,, 26
	335	then	,,	them	,,	,, 30
	335	seruice	,,	seruise	,,	,, 30
III, iii, s.d.	1	*Spendall &*	,,	*Spendall and*	,,	,, 32
	2	but	,,	bnt	,,	,, 35
s.p.	6	*Spend.*	,,	*Spend*	,,	,, catchwd.
				ˣ ˣ		
Sig. E3ᵛ R.T.		*EASTWARD*	,,	*EASTWARD*[1]	,,	
III, iii, s.p.	6	*Spend.*	,,	*Spend,*	,,	Sig. E3ᵛ 1
	9	Pewter	1, 9*	Pewter,	,,	,, 4
	10	And	,,	Aud	,,	,, 5

[1] 'x' above letter = swash cap.

13	commaund	,,	command	,,	,,	8
14	snare	,,	share	,,	,,	9
17	Country	,,	Conntry	,,	,,	12
28	Gould	,,	Gold	,,	,,	26
30	stick	,,	sticke	,,	,,	28
31	Cappes	,,	Capps	,,	,,	28
32	and| and groates	,,	and groates|	,,	,, 29–30	
36	thē	,,	then	,,	,,	35
37	shal	,,	shall	,,	,,	35
37	Sergeants, or Cour-|tiers	,,	Sargeants, or| Courtiers	,,	,, 35–36	
38	Intelligencers,	,,	Intellingencers.	,,	,,	36

38–41   onely a few industrious| Scots perhaps, who
indeed are disperst ouer the face of the|
whole earth. But as for them, there are no
greater friends to| English-
in 1, 9*   36–catchwd.

See crit. note 48   Then for your| meanes to aduance-
ment, there, it is simple, and not preposte-|
rously   36–catchwd.
the rest

Sig. E4ʳ R.T. *EASTWARD*ˣ   1, 9*   *EASTWARD*ˣ the rest
III, iii, 41–5 English men and *England*, when they are out
an't, in the| world, then they are. And for
my part, I would a hundred| thousand of
'hem were there, for wee are all one
Countrey-| men now, yee know; and wee
should finde ten times more| comfort of
them there, then wee doe heere.
1, 9*   Sig. E4ʳ 1–5

48	a Noble man	,,	any other officer	the rest	,,	8
48	Slaue; you	,,	Slaue. You	,,	,,	9
49	Pandar: To	1, 9*	*Pandar*. To	,,	,,	10
49	riches	,,	Riches,	,,	,,	10
50	fortune enough,	,,	Forune inough	,,	,,	10
50	villanie	,,	Villany	,,	,,	11
51	wit.	,,	wit. Besides, there, we shall haue| no more Law then Conscience and not too much of either;| serue God inough, eate and drink inough, and *inough is as| good as a Feast.* the rest			see crit. note 48
53	indefferent	1, 9*	indifferent	the rest	Sig. E4ʳ	13
54	And if	,,	And If	,,	,,	14
56	continually	,,	continuall	,,	,,	16

	56	tell	,,	till	,,	,,	16
	57	*Uirginia*	,,	*Virginia*	,,	,,	17
	57	See	,,	See,	,,	,,	17
s.d.	58	*Petronell.*	,,	*Petronell with his Followers.*	,,	,,	18
III, iii.	59	Now	,,	Nowe	,,	,,	20
	60	*Drawer,*	,,	*Drawer.*	,,	,,	21
	60	mirthe	,,	mirth	,,	,,	22
	61	pretty	,,	prety	,,	,,	23
	62	companie	,,	company	,,	,,	24
	68	Collonell	,,	Colonell	,,	,,	31
	68	*it.*	,,	*it,*	,,	,,	32
	69	one,	,,	one	,,	,,	33
	70	touche,	,,	touch,	,,	,,	34
	70	yee	,,	ye	,,	,,	35
s.p.	72	*Spend,*	,,	*Enter*	,,	,, catchwd.	
	72	forhead	1, 9*	forehead	,,	Sig. E4^v	1
	73	both.	,,	both,	,,	,,	2
	74	maister	,,	Maister	,,	,,	4
	76	god	,,	God	,,	,,	6
	78	Coun-| saile	,,	Coun-| saile,	,,	,,	8–9
	78	Maister	,,	M.			
	80	Maister	,,	M.	,,	,,	10
	80	draw| us	,,	drawe us|	,,	,,	11–12
	81	Captaine| Seagull	,,	Captain *Seagull*|	,,	,,	12–13
	82	a| pricke	,,	a pricke	,,	,,	13–14
s.p.	84	*Pet.*	,,	*Sea.*	,,	,,	14
	87	,Maister *Bramble*	,,	M. *Bramble,*	,,	,,	17
	87	you| shall	,,	you shal|	,,	,,	17–18
	89	so maister	,,	so, M.	,,	,,	19
	89	he	,,	hee	,,	,,	19
	89	pledge	,,	pleadge	,,	,,	19
s.p.	91	*Secur.*	,,	*Secu.*	,,	,,	21
s.d.	92	*disguisd.*	,,	*disguis'd*	,,	,,	21
	92	do	,,	doe	,,	,,	22
s.p.	93	*Quick:*	,,	*Quick.*	,,	,,	23
	93	Cosin,	,,	Cosen,	,,	,,	27
	97	me	,,	mee	,,	,,	27
	98	me	,,	mee	,,	,,	28
	98	entreate	,,	entreat	,,	,,	28
	100	Maister	,,	M.	,,	,,	30
	103	you	1, 3, 6, 8, 9*, 10	*you*	,,	,,	33
s.p.	104	*Secur.*	1, 9*	*Secu.*	,,	,,	34
	104	counsaile, Maister	,,	Counsaile, M.	,,	,,	34
s.p.	106	*Quic.*	1, 9*	*Quick.*	,,	,,	36
	106	time;	,,	time,	,,	,,	36

s.p. 108	*Secur.*	,,	*Secu.*	,,	,,	38
108	her,	,,	her	,,	,,	38
108	be	,,	bee	,,	,,	38

148	hant	3, 10, 11	haunt	the rest	Sig. F1ᵛ	1
168	*Cuckholds*	,,	*Cuckolds*	,,	,,	22
171	learned	,,	learn'd	,,	,,	24
180	*Exit.*	,,	[omitted]	,,	,,	34
III, iv, 5	aboate	,,	a boate	,,	Sig. F2ʳ	7
IV, i, 25	thee yet; a	,,	thee; yet a	,,	,,	36
54	another	1, 4, 7, 9	a nother	,,	Sig. F2ᵛ	29
103	Thanck	3, 10, 11	Thanke	,,	Sig. F3ᵛ	3
110	omenous	,,	ominous	,,	,,	10
s.d. 113	*Euter*	,,	*Enter*	,,	,,	12
122	rootes,	,,	rootes.	,,	,,	22
129	Bote	,,	Boate	,,	,,	29
s.p. 138	*Pat.*	,,	*Pet.*	,,	Sig. F4ʳ	1
144	See?	,,	See!	,,	,,	6
145	heres	,,	hers	2, 5, 6		
			here	the rest	,,	7
145	Gentleman;I	3, 11	Gentleman; I	,,	,,	7
149	'hem	2, 3, 5	hem	,,	,,	11
152	Pray you	,,	Pray you,	,,	,,	13
153	*davoir*	3, 10, 11	*d'avoir*	,,	,,	14
153	*infortunes,*	,,	*infortunes?*	,,	,,	14
154	*souffril'*	2, 5, 8, 10, 11	*souffri'l*	,,	,,	15
s.p. 156	1. *Gen.*	3, 10, 11	1. *Gent.*	,,	,,	17
157	*Monsieuer*	,,	*Monsieur*	,,	,,	18
s.p. 157	[omitted]	,,	*Pet.*	,,	,,	18
s.p. 159	2 *Gen.*	,,	2 *Gent.*	,,	,,	20
160	y'are,	,,	y'are	,,	,,	22
161	are you	,,	are you,	,,	,,	22
163	ith,	,,	ith'	,,	,,	25
166	bote	,,	boate	,,	,,	28
166-7	Farewell, farewell,	,,	Farewel, farewel,	,,	,,	28
221	*Ahcyme*	9, 6	*Achyme*	,,	Sig. G1ʳ	5
229	shall asigne	,,	shal, assigne	,,	,,	13
s.d. 231	*Wynifred,*	,,	*Wynifrid,*	,,	,,	15
231	nerae,	,,	neare,	,,	,,	18
236	k epe	,,	keepe	,,	,,	21
240	for	,,	for,	,,	,,	25
IV, ii, 12	ad,n	3, 4, 6, 8, 9	and	2, 5, 7, 1		
			catch cropped	10, 11	catchwd.	

	86	Brother,i	6, 9	Brother,)	the rest	Sig. G2ᵛ 29
s.p.	103	*Gold.*	,,	*Gould.*	,,	Sig. G3ʳ 8
s.d.	108	[crit. n.]				
		Golding	,,	*Goulding*	,,	,, 13
	134	feather	9, 10	feather,	,,	Sig. G3ᵛ 2
	216	Thing.	6, 9	Thing,	,,	Sig. G4ᵛ 2
	224	withhis	,,	with his	,,	,, 10
	228	so	,,	to	,,	,, 14
	245	*into a*	9	*in a*	,,	,, 30
	247	*Petrionell*	,,	*Petronell*	,,	,, 31
	249	thē	,,	thē:	,,	,, 33
	284	fortune	3, 7, 9	fortune	,,	Sig, H1ʳ 27
V, iii,	12	me	3, 10	me,	,,	Sig. I1ʳ 2
	36	Why,	1, 10	Why.	,,	,, 26
	82	co mmit	1, 7	co mm t	,,	Sig. I1ᵛ 32
	99	relent	1, 9	relent,	,,	Sig. I2ʳ 10
V, iv,	7	your	1, 7	our	,,	,, 29
V, v,	166–7	restitu	1, 11, 7	reisttu	,,	Sig. I4ʳ catchwd.

Printed in Great Britain by
The Garden City Press Limited, Letchworth, Hertfordshire SG6 1JS